CW01236911

American
GHOST BASES of
EASTERN ENGLAND

Martin W. Bowman

HALSGROVE

First published in Great Britain in 2019
Copyright © Martin W. Bowman

All rights reserved. No part of this publication may be reproduced, stored in a retrieval system, or transmitted in any form or by any means without the prior permission of the copyright holder.

British Library Cataloguing-in-Publication Data
A CIP record for this title is available from the British Library

ISBN 978 0 85704 340 5

Halsgrove
Halsgrove House,
Ryelands Business Park,
Bagley Road, Wellington, Somerset TA21 9PZ
Tel: 01823 653777   Fax: 01823 216796
email: sales@halsgrove.com

Part of the Halsgrove group of companies
Information on all Halsgrove titles is available at:
www.halsgrove.com

Printed and bound in India by Parksons Graphics Pvt Ltd

CONTENTS

PROLOGUE 4

1. A CORNER OF ENGLAND THAT WILL BE FOREVER AMERICA 5
*If there are ghosts they surely haunt the East Anglian wartime airfields.
I will admit to having felt a 'presence' on the back of my neck and down my spine on more than one occasion.*

2. WE'RE HERE TO WIN THE WAR FOR YOU 8
This was December, Nineteen Forty Two. He said: 'We're here to win the war for you.'

3. RETURN TO ARCHBURY 19
Stop making plans. Forget about going home. Consider yourselves already dead.

4. MOVIE STARS: MYTHS IN THE MISTS OF TIME 27
When the legend becomes fact, print the legend.

5. CASTLES IN THE AIR 37
*A desire, idea, or plan that is unlikely to ever be realized; a visionary project or scheme;
a daydream, an idle fancy, a near impossibility.*

6. CHRISTMAS IN THE ETO 54
*'No one could ever forget those Christmas parties for the orphans and evacuee children, with the kids yelling
and gobbling ice cream, sitting on our shoulders and singing for us.... going home along the lane clutching
armfuls of toys and candy, chewing gum and biscuits. Fifteen hundred we had at one party.*

7. GHOST FIELDS OF LITTLE AMERICA 62
*'A pilot told his bunkmate, a staff officer who worked in the control tower, that if he was killed he would
come back to haunt the tower.'*

8. THE STATELY HOMES OF THE EIGHTH IN ENGLAND 78
*Major John D. Davis commanding the 401st Bomb Squadron, 91st Bomb Group at Bassingbourn
later married Lieutenant Helen Pierson, an Army Nurse stationed at the nearby 163rd General Hospital at Wimpole Hall.*

9. 'ARTISTIC LICENSE' 84
*'We were flying somebody else's plane, the Keystone Mama. I turned my flashlight on the brown lady
with no brassiere, painted on the side and decided they were short of artists at this base.'*

10. FLYING TO VICTORY 116
Hermann Goering said he knew the air war was lost when he saw the bombers over the capital with their P-51 escorts.

VERNACULAR 126

PROLOGUE

This is where I came in!

The author pictured at Deenethorpe in the early 1970s.
Sadly, the tower was demolished in the spring of 1999.

1. A CORNER OF ENGLAND THAT WILL BE FOREVER AMERICA

American troops, or 'GIs' as they were known because of their own derisive term of 'General Issue', began arriving in war-weary Britain in the months immediately after Pearl Harbor. The 'Yanks' as they were universally known, came from the big cities and the backwoods, up state and down town, from California to Connecticut, the Deep South to Dixie, Delaware to Dakota, Frisco to Florida, Mid-West to Maine, the mighty Mississip' to Missouri, New York, New England, Ohio and Hawaii, the Pacific, 'Philly' and the Rockies to the Rio Grande, from Texas to Tallahassee, Wyoming, Wisconsin, the 'Windy City' and way beyond. The parochial parishes of England and the Americans themselves were in for a culture shock.

Martin W. Bowman

When I was a teenager I investigated the myriad number of airfields clustered around my fair city of Norwich, often taking to my scooter to explore these talked-about places which had just been featured in a book called *The Mighty Eighth* by one Roger Freeman. Having previously thought that all of the bases were occupied by the RAF bomber and fighter squadrons in WW2, I was intrigued to discover that they had in fact been 'invaded' and taken over by crews from every state of the Union who flew and worked on the 'heavy bombers' and 'pursuits' of the US 8th and 9th Air Forces and in headquarters, hospitals, rest homes and suchlike. The culture shock on people from both sides of the Atlantic caused by the influx of the many thousands of Americans must have been enormous. The locals, who had only encountered the otherwise unfamiliar New York-ese and Texas drawl on the silver screen in cowboy films in British cinemas, gradually became accustomed to the 'friendly invasion' and the 'funny' accents. Whilst they would never get used to warm beer the 'Yanks' or the 'GIs' as they were known, (because they considered themselves 'General Issue') ultimately came to terms with the litany of local dialects and the parochial and often quaint English lifestyle, which many thought came straight out of the storybooks. Off base sojourns called 'pubbing missions' and 'R & R' (Rest and Recuperation) helped cement relationships. They dated and married their English sweethearts and broke the hearts of many more as they roamed far and wide, from London to Liverpool, to Cambridge, Oxford, Stratford-On-Avon and Edinburgh, Glasgow and Belfast and a hundred other places.

At first my friends and I sortied to bases near Norwich because we did not immediately have the resources to range further afield and precious little film for our basic little Kodak 'Instamatic' cameras to record what we saw.

My co-conspirators thoughts were of finding machine guns, ammunition and bits of bombs but like the famous Egyptologist, Howard Carter, my head was turned in another direction. I too soon discovered 'wonderful things' – No, not a 3,000 year old tomb of the pharaohs adorned with hieroglyphics or elegant paintings set in amber. Nor slim limbed figures in precisely curled wigs, shining gold necklaces and fresh green fruits and leaves from the field, all arranged in simple harmony. Instead I found 1940s' 'Varga girls' and Gil Elvegren 'pin ups', American cartoon characters and murals and much more to behold. 'Wall art' we now call it. I was hooked and have been ever since.

It led me, in the early 1970s, to begin compiling stories of the young GIs and their aircraft that populated and flew from, these 'Fields of Little America'. I tried to record the wall art images for posterity but I was unable to turn back time for long. Life's more important matters intruded for a few years and when I re-acquainted myself with the wartime bases armed with an expensive camera or two it was almost too late. These remote places had been ravaged by the almost biblical winters and heavy rains that pummel our region annually and the infrastructure that survived had been claimed by business concerns and converted while farmers ploughed up many runways and taxiways to grow more crops. Few people, if any were interested in historic preservation. Thankfully, this changed over time. Now returning siblings of past heroes are amazed and heartened to find scores of worthy aviation museums, memorials and historical tribute sites at places such as Thorpe Abbotts and Debach, Hethel and Shipdham to name but a few, scattered in a swathe throughout Eastern England.

I became familiar with exciting films ('movies' the Americans call them) like *Twelve o'clock High, The Longest Day, The Dam Busters* and *633 Squadron* and began to taste 'the real thing' throughout the 1970s when I was able to meet hundreds of 8th Air Force veterans ('Jimmy' Stewart was the only movie star among them) who returned in their hundreds year on year, until old age and infirmities ended their humble pilgrimage. They had survived early adulthood, flying combat missions, some ending up incarcerated in stalags throughout the Reich and all having to endure the primitive, rudimentary and often freezing conditions on the bases of East Anglia.

Investigative writers and historians rarely suffer danger and privation but my boyhood dreams finally came true with flights in famous bombers such as the Flying Fortress, Liberator, B-52 and Lancaster and two trips into war zones in a C-130 as well as being 'arrested' on , and catapulted off a US carrier *John F. Kennedy* in a C-2 Greyhound in the Mediterrenean. Someone has to do it! But while you are only 'a fly on the wall' let's make no bones about it; if the plane gets squashed – so do you.

Soaking up the atmosphere of the old bases and immersing oneself in living history are far more comfortable pursuits. And while, over 200 published books later, the fascination engendered in those early years has not diminished, my missions of re-discovery have long since been equalled by visits to the Valley of the Kings, Karnak, Cairo, Colditz and Berlin to name but a few. But while re-discovering and photographing ancient Egyptian wall paintings in underground tombs is enticing (and open to arrest and a fine), re-discovering and recording wartime artwork in deserted wartime buildings has always held more allure for me than ancient archaeology.

The often remote and quiet heart of the East Anglian countryside where Flying Fortress, Liberator and Marauder bombers and Mustang, Thunderbolt and Lightning fighters once flew, are corners of a 'foreign field' that will be forever America. In the words of Rupert Brooke, '*Her sights and sounds; dreams happy as her day; And laughter, learnt of friends; and gentleness, In hearts at peace, under an English heaven.*'

It is on these 'Fields of Little America' that our story starts like all the good old Hollywood movies, in flashback.

Welcome to the War.

Thorpe Abbotts Tower Museum. (Author)

2. WE'RE HERE TO WIN THE WAR FOR YOU

Yankee Doodle went to town, A-riding on a pony, He stuck a feather in his hat. And called it macaroni.

Captain Charles C. Kegelman and his crew in front of their Douglas A-20 in the 15th Light Bombardment Squadron – the first USAAF unit to fly a mission from England when on 4 July 1942 at the RAF grass airfield at Swanton Morley in Norfolk six Bostons flown by RAF pilots and six American took off for attacks on four German airfields in Holland. One RAF and two all-American-crewed aircraft were shot down. Of the four airfield targets, only one was attacked successfully.

'Achtung, feindliche Flugzeuge!' Jagdfuhrer or Fighter Control, Holland had picked up four three-plane elements heading across the North Sea. Immediately, Luftwaffe fighter units were alerted. German radar had picked up twelve US-built Douglas Boston twin-engined medium bombers thundering low across the North Sea to four airfield targets in Holland. Six of the aircraft carried RAF crews while American crews of the 15th Bomb Squadron (Light) manned the other half dozen. Significantly, it was 4 July 1942 – American Independence Day – and the first time American airmen had flown in US-built bombers against a German target. Contrary to folklore they were not the revered Flying Fortresses that many Hollywood producers would have us believe won the war on their own. (In August 1942 Major General Ira C. Eaker, Commander of VIIIth Bomber Command had just three operational B-17 Flying Fortress Groups – 92nd, 97th and 301st. The 97th Bomb Group would not fly the first heavy bomber mission, to Lille until 17 August.)

At Swanton Morley airfield in Norfolk on 1 July Captain Charles C. Kegelman, acting squadron commander put all nine of his American pilots' names in a hat. Six were marked with a 'yes' and three marked 'no'. The 'lucky' six later discovered that they would fly a famous 4

The author flying inverted over Swanton Morley airfield in a Yak-52 piloted by John Carter.

July raid to German airfields in Holland with six RAF Boston crews. It seemed a little ironic that they had been pressed into taking part in an American Independence Day celebration commemorating the severance of ties between their two countries. Four flights of three aircraft were to attack four fighter airdromes at De Kooy, Bergen Alkmaar, Valkenburg and Haamstede at low-level and in broad daylight.

At De Kooy intense flak prevented all three Bostons from bombing and one American-crewed aircraft was hit and crashed on the beach killing three crew. The bombardier survived and was taken prisoner. Kegelman's Boston received a hit in the starboard engine and burst into flames and the propeller flew off. Kegelman's right wing tip struck the ground and the fuselage actually bounced on the surface of the aerodrome, tearing a hole in the belly of the bomber. Lifting the Boston back into the air on one engine, Kegelman headed for the Channel, returning fire on a flak tower at Den Helder airfield before heading for England. The engine fire went out over the Channel and Kegelman continued home to Swanton Morley hugging the waves across the North Sea.

At Swanton Morley the first returning Boston landed at 0814 hours. During the next forty minutes the others landed. The last to touch down was Kegelman, who despite the loss of one engine made a good landing and taxied to the control tower before shutting down. Inspection of his aircraft revealed scratch marks on the belly of his Boston where he had touched the ground. The experienced 226 Squadron crews were all of the same opinion that the flak encountered on the raid was the worst the squadron had ever experienced. Three American-crewed Bostons in total were missing. At Bergen-Alkmaar one was hit by a heavy shell and hit the ground right in the middle of the airfield and 'flew into a million pieces'. After bombing, a Me109 shot down one of the others into the sea. The third Boston was shot down attacking De Kooy and crashed on a beach. Only the bombardier survived and he was taken prisoner.

One returning American pilot said: 'General Eaker, General Duncan and Beaman were there at the start and finish and didn't look so happy at the finish. They must have thought it was a 'piece of cake' until three turned up shot down – two being American. Thusly, we celebrated Independence Day!'

In the middle of Ambassador John C. Winant's Fourth of July party at the Court of St James in London, Captain Harry C. Butcher, General Eisenhower's naval aide passed the results of the first American raid to General Eisenhower. Of the four airfield targets, only one had been attacked successfully. Of the six American crews taking part, only one had engaged the Luftwaffe with good results.

'So You're Going to Fly In England'.

These lines are dedicated to a man
I met in Glasgow, an American.
He was an Army officer, not old,
In the late twenties. If the truth were told
A great deal younger then he thought he was
I mention this ironically because,
After we'd had a drink or two, he said
Something so naive, so foolish, that I fled.
This was December, Nineteen Forty Two.
He said: We're here to win the war for you.'

Lines to An American officer, Nóel Coward

Spitfire Mk.VB in the 309th Fighter Squadron, 78th Fighter Group, 8th Air Force at Membury (High Ercall), on 15 March 1943. The 31st and 52nd Fighter Groups arrived in England during the summer of 1942. Each group was composed of three squadrons of sixteen fighters but the US fighter groups arrived without their P-39 Airacobras. A joint American-Canadian fighter sweep by six Spitfires over Gravelines, France on 26 July resulted in the loss of one fighter and the capture of the group's executive officer.

'BEHIND EVERY BOMBER is an airdrome, from which it sets out and to which it must return. Behind every airdrome is a base that houses the men who work on the airdrome from which the bomber flies. Behind every base lie months of planning, thousands of man-hours of labor and millions of dollars of material and equipment – all of which must be expended before the men can move into the base and the base can run the airdrome and the airdrome can put the bomber into the air.

'And so to be able to bomb you first have to build. In the European Theater the heavy-bomber base covers several hundred acres of farmland. The core of each base is the airdrome, crisscrossed by 150-foot-wide concrete runways. A perimeter track, for moving planes around the field, skins the inner border and concrete dispersal points on which the bombers are parked between missions dot the fringes of the area. Scattered around the airdrome are the 'sites' on which the personnel are housed. On the edge of the field proper are placed the administration buildings, the shops, and one or two, large hangars for heavy repair work. Dovetailing into the irregular outline of the area are the neighboring farms.

'Such a station may serve as a base for approximately fifty heavy bombers. Twenty-five hundred officers and men fly, service, and repair the planes and carry on the administrative tasks of the station. The sum of the materials and labor, which go into the construction of this combination town, factory and transport terminus, is a factor, which looms large in the development of any bombing program.

'They came in no uncertain fashion with their jeeps, their superior uniforms, their big mouths and their big hearts.'

George Greengrass, a soldier at Gibraltar Barracks, Bury St Edmunds.

US airmen on bicycles arriving at their 97th Bomb Group hardstand at Grafton Underwood where B-17 *Berlin Sleeper II* awaits.

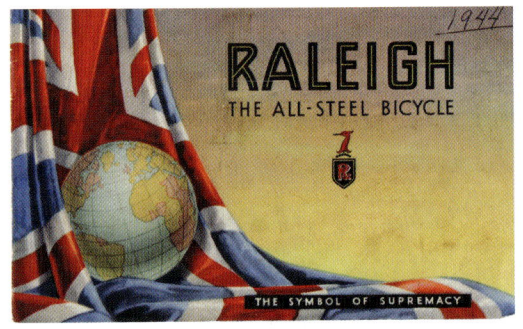

A 1944 advertisement for Raleigh bicycles.

'We're a new B-17 crew just in from the States, temporarily stationed at this Army Air Force Replacement Depot. What they call a 'repple depple' – fifty or so Nissen huts about twenty yards long, shaped like long barrels sliced in half lengthwise and plopped down in the countryside here in Bovingdon, fifteen miles west of London. Lots of hurried comings and goings with no-one paying too much attention to us. Just another dumb-ass crew. Ten guys, raw as stumps and not half as smart waiting to be assigned any day now to operations at an 8th Air Force Bomb Group somewhere in England. We goof off as best we can from all the "hurry up and wait" calls, the gas mask and air raid drills and the medics insisting we take every one of our shots all over again. Most of the time we hang around with the other new crews spreading **** just about as far as it will go, mostly about girls and sex, though I'd bet that the guys talking the most haven't had any much more than me and I've had zip.'

A Real Good War **by Sam Halpert**

Yankee-Doodle in the 97th Bomb Group, which was flown by Colonel Frank Armstrong and carried Brigadier General Ira C. Eaker to Rouen on 17 August 1942 on the first B-17 Flying Fortress mission of the war.

'To Bomber Command's engineers this problem presents itself in terms of war schedules, material priorities, and weather. It is also a problem of multiplication of the fifty airplanes on each station; twenty may be dispatched on each mission, the others being held in reserve. Thus it takes fifteen bases to supply the bombers for a 300-plane raid and fifty bases to implement a 1000-plane attack. It takes 1,500,000 man-hours and $5,000,000 worth of construction to prepare each bomber base for combat operations. It takes 640,000 square yards of concrete slab to construct the runways, the perimeter tracks, and the foundations for some 400 buildings, which must be erected on one station - this concrete would form a road eighteen feet wide and sixty miles long. It takes bulldozers and trucks and concrete mixers and wheelbarrows and shovels and picks and sand and gravel, and tar and tractors; it takes transits and tarvia, levels and steam shovels, brick and glass and mortar and wire and pipe; it means telephones and drainage tile, paint and roofing paper, Nissen huts and bathtubs, flood lights and telephone poles; it demands laborers – who must be too young or too old for military service – and electricians and shovel operators and plumbers and carpenters and draftsmen and strong young girls to drive the laden trucks. Hundreds of tons of rubble are required for subgrade foundations – rubble formed when Germans bombed British cities. Warehouses, theaters, churches, barracks, offices, and machine shops have to be built. Water, electrical and sewage systems must be laid down, and all this must be multiplied by ten or twenty of fifty, depending upon the size of the bomber fleet.'

Men, Mud and Machines, Target Germany.

The first *Alabama Exterminator* in the 97th Bomb Group crashed on a rocky beach in Greenland on 27 June 1942 en route to England. *Alabama Exterminator II* was used as a ferry navigation aircraft until it was transferred to the 384 Bomb Group at Grafton Underwood on 4 June 1943 and used as a target tug and 'hack'.

Bringing in the sheaves at a B-17 Fortress base in East Anglia. Living accommodation, mess halls, hospital, clubs and other facilities were nestled in among farms, trees, barns, cow pastures and thatched cottages. Crews were impressed by the neat, compact countryside. There was every shade of green one could imagine and the tranquillity it conveyed belied the anxiety and apprehension that was always prevalent. Crews were again impressed with the airfields 5 miles apart in every direction; there was an airfield about every 36 square miles.

B-24 Liberators in the 93rd Bomb Group at Hardwick in flight. 'Ted's Travelling Circus' as it was later known and the 44th 'Flying Eightballs' were the first two Liberator groups in the ETO (European Theatre of Operations), in 1943.

'The Intelligence Room is filled with shifting movement now. The movement is intent and purposeful. It is resolute but glum – for this is the hour when men should sleep, not plan death and destruction. Outside, the station is still dark and quiet. The moon is down and the breeze has died and a thin sheet of haze lies over the runways. There is the faint and acrid smell of coal smoke in the air. In the Operations Room the Watch Officer is checking crew lists with a Squadron Commander. At another desk the Group Navigator marks a precise cross at a point on the North Sea and slides his parallel rulers down toward the German coast … 0300 hours on a chill June morning is no time to get up. Group 500 does get up – with howls and curses, in deliberate silence, or with laughter. Each man faces the black morning in his own 'fashion, for each knows that Group 500 is going out. The weather has held. The combat crews – the pilots, the copilots, the navigators, the bombardiers, and the gunners – get into their flying outfits. First, the heavy underwear, then the bright-blue, electrically heated 'zoot suit' of flannel, O.D. [olive drab] trousers or fleece-lined leather pants, and a sheepskin jacket No two dress alike, each man catering to his whims and the requirements of his post. Heated gloves and boots in one hand and Mae West and helmet in the other, they're ready for the truck to the mess hall.

'By 0330 the barracks housing the combat and the maintenance crews are emptied and the mess halls filled. The station is awakening now, as the intimation of action spreads like an ever-widening ripple. Across the rolling plain of central England this gradual stirring is duplicated at each Group assigned to Mission 95. The tempo quickens; a note of urgency is for the first time apparent in the movement. At Group 500 the Flying Control Officer is bending over a plan of the field, plotting the marshaling of his forces with the deliberateness of a choreographer – each plane in its place on the perimeter track, each off at thirty-second intervals, and each in its place at 5,000 feet…'

Mission 95, Target Germany.

B-17 bomber crews in the 401st Bomb Group look over a P-51 Mustang in the 354th Fighter Group from Boxted at Deenethorpe airfield on 27 December 1943. The 354th was known as the Pioneer Mustang Group and was the first to fly the P-51B Mustang in combat.

Martin B-26 Marauders in the 322nd Bomb Group (Medium) at Andrews Field in Essex. Some farms with thatched cottages and open straw stooks, here intermingled with Nissen huts, which were spotted about in clusters, some under tall beeches and chestnuts. Other of the farms and their woods and hedgerows were levelled for runways and hard standings. Airbases were completely mixed with farm, field and spinney. Pheasants crowed near the barracks sites and rabbits came out in late summer evenings. They could be a lovely spot, even to homesick Amercians.

The USAAF high command believed in their own mistaken prophecy that their B-17s and B-24s, heavily armed so as not to need escort fighters, could, in broad daylight, penetrate even the strongest defences and achieve 'pickle barrel' bombing accuracy (i.e. have the ability to drop a bomb in a pickle barrel from 25,000 feet) that bombardiers had performed in the clear skies of Texas and the southern States. But by September, losses were on the increase and bombing accuracy having been poor, orders were that the Fortresses would bomb the U-boat bases on the French coast from 7,000-8,000 feet! In theory, these heights were between the low and high flak. At Thurleigh, Colonel 'Chip' Overacker the 3067th Bomb Group CO reacted furiously to the Field Order. As soon as it appeared on the teletype machine at the base, he telephoned HQ, VIIIth BC, to protest but nothing could change the decision. Overacker responded that if his crews had to fly the mission then so would he and that he'd lead them! His four squadron commanders joined him on the mission. It was a disaster. In seconds, three Fortresses were shot down in rapid succession by flak with the loss of 22 crew. Several other B-17s, including Overacker's, which was very badly damaged, were in bad shape and some barely made it home.

On 23 November, the 306th lost four B-17s to head-on attacks by fighters. On 25 November, the Group was removed from the battle order for a month. There then followed another week's rest from combat, missions resuming on the 19th with a long, unescorted mission to Romilly, 100 miles southeast of Paris. The 'unlucky' 367th 'Clay Pigeons' Bomb Squadron lost three B-17s and 29 crew. This squadron's original complement of nine crews now numbered just three. At Thurleigh, respiratory ailments were rife and the enlisted men grumbled about unsanitary conditions and poor food. Every army has its complainers and backsliders but feeling sorry for yourself is not a condition that can be tolerated for long, especially if higher command identifies that the condition is widespread and constitutes a serious morale problem. By early January 1943 the 306th Bomb Group had a new CO.

All of these events were to inspire one of the greatest war novels of all time.

3. RETURN TO ARCHBURY

'Things are not going well up there. I think we ought to take a look around. Respiratory ailments are rife and the enlisted men are grumbling about unsanitary conditions and the poor food on offer. Every army has its complainers and backsliders but feeling sorry for oneself is not a condition than can be tolerated for long, especially if higher command identifies that the condition is widespread and constitutes a morale problem.'

General Ira C. Eaker on his visit to the 306th Bomb Group at Thurleigh on 6 January 1943

Twelve O'clock High is one of the great war movies that Hollywood used to make. In 1946, while many people's thoughts turned to peace, others were still thinking of war. WW2 bomber pilot and screenwriter, Beirne Lay, who was born on 1 September 1909, was working for MGM on *Above and Beyond*, the story of Colonel Paul Tibbets, the pilot of the *Enola Gay*, the B-29 Superfortress that dropped the atomic bomb on Hiroshima. Lay enlisted in the United States Army in July 1932 and began pilot training at Randolph Field, Texas. In June 1933 he earned his pilot's wings and was commissioned a second lieutenant in the Army Reserve at Kelly Field, Texas. Lay began his writing career while still on active duty by submitting rebuttal articles and pieces on aviation in general. In November 1935 he left active duty but remained a Reserve officer, promoted to 1st lieutenant on 16 August 1936. His autobiographical book *I Wanted Wings* was published in 1937. He sold the film rights to Paramount Pictures and helped write the screenplay for a film adaptation.

In 1939 Lay returned to active duty at his own request, as a flying instructor in Chino, California. The publication of *I Wanted Wings* brought Lay to the attention of Colonel Ira Eaker, chief of the Air Corps Information Division and himself a writer. Lay was soon promoted to captain and he worked primarily as a speechwriter for

Beirne Lay Junior.

General Henry H. Arnold, Chief of the Army Air Corps. In January 1942 Eaker was made brigadier general and went to England to create the Eighth Air Force. Lay was Eaker's Eighth Air Force Historian and Film Unit commander. By February 1944 Lay was a lieutenant colonel in command of the 487th Bomb Group at Lavenham. On 11 May he led his Liberator group to Troyes, France on its fourth combat mission. The 487th encountered heavy flak near Châteaudun, the location of a Luftwaffe fighter airfield and both Lay's B-24 and that of his deputy commander were shot down. Lay parachuted from his aircraft near Coulonges-les-Sablons and was hidden by members of the French Resistance.

Lay returned to Hollywood after the war and he was approached by Sy Bartlett, another Eighth Air Force veteran, who as a major had been General Spaatz's aide, to collaborate on the novel-screenplay project which became *Twelve O'clock High*. Bartlett was now working as a screenwriter at 20th Century-Fox Studios and he wanted Lay to co-write the screenplay on the movie about the air war. In 1948, with the novel *Twelve O'clock High* nearing publication, Louis D. 'Bud' Lighton, a producer at Fox, immediately became very interested in the possibility of a screenplay of the same name. Studio head Darryl F. Zanuck promptly purchased the movie rights. Zanuck hired Henry King, an accomplished pilot, as the movie's director, who, together with Bartlett and Lay, greatly refined the overlong script and arrived at a highly polished final draft. The central theme would be the gradual and ultimate destruction of 'General Frank Savage' played superbly by Gregory Peck, who commands the fictionalized '918th Bomb Group', which Lay arrived at by taking the actual 306th Bomb Group that flew from Thurleigh in Bedfordshire and multiplying it by three.

The story begins in the present day and then in dramatic flashback, returns the moviegoer to 'Archbury', a parochial and fictitious 8th Air Force airfield in Bedfordshire in 1943 in surroundings hardly changed since Dickens' time.

In 1949, now overgrown and at peace, the weapons of war having been turned into ploughshares, our narrator, Dean Jagger, aka Major Harvey Stovall, the 918th Bomb Group's wartime Ground Executive, returns from America on business in London and by chance catches sight of 'his' much revered old wartime Toby jug in the window of a little antique shop. Though the better jugs are inside he buys the battered old pot for 'ten bob', catches a train to 'Bedfordshire' and cycles to 'Archbury' airfield with the prized possession in the front basket. He surveys the unfolding scene of cows and broken concrete runways and the film set control tower of Lilliputian dimensions (where the actors would have to be barely six inches high) when suddenly we are seamlessly and dramatically transported back to takeoff time and the crack of a Very pistol signalling the 'Forts' to start engines followed by the parting of the grass as Wright Cyclones roar in unison (although we don't see them), to be replaced by the barely audible strains of *Don't Sit Under the Apple Tree With Anyone But Me; Bless Em All* and *We are poor little lambs Who have lost our way. Baa! Baa! Baa! We are little black sheep Who have gone astray...*

Then cue the return of the 'Forts' of the 'Hard Luck Group' in the overhead, throttled back and descending carefully, a Very pistol shot denoting wounded aboard. There is a belly crash landing, which was performed by veteran Hollywood stunt pilot Paul Mantz during filming, largely shot at Eglin AFB, Florida and Ozark, Alabama from February to 1 July 1949 using a dozen ex-wartime B-17s. Then, like the opening scene in M*A*S*H, a khaki coloured ambulance appears and, stopping beside the open rear door, with the words *Where Angels and Generals fear to tread* stencilled above it, waits while one of the gunners without an arm and the co-pilot who has been hit in the back of the head with his brain showing are stretchered into the back.

The storyline draws upon the 306th Bomb Group's troubled early combat history flying from Thurleigh in Bedfordshire and its effect on the combat crews. Some characterizations are amalgams of many actual personalities. such as Generals Ira C. Eaker (portrayed as Major General Patrick Pritchard) and Frank A. Armstrong Jr., a West Pointer, who had been given command of the troubled 306th Bomb Group on 4 January 1943 vice 'Chip' Overacker with the task of rebuilding the group's shattered morale. 'Likable, decent, Colonel Keith Davenport' (aka 'Chip' Overacker) played by Gary Merrill, is popular with his crews, but he cannot prevent the high losses, delegate, nor impose the strong discipline needed to change things. He is replaced by resolute hard taskmaster and West Pointer Frank Savage, aka Gregory Peck. Savage uncompromisingly sweeps info office not so much as a new broom, but like a whirlwind. Gradually, he earns his crew's grudging respect, but not their devotion. He does not seek it. He requires only their obedience instilled by military discipline, both in the air and on the ground. Training, training and more training follow, until the 918th's poor formation flying is improved.

Dean Jagger aka Major Harvey Stovall is reunited with his Toby Jug.

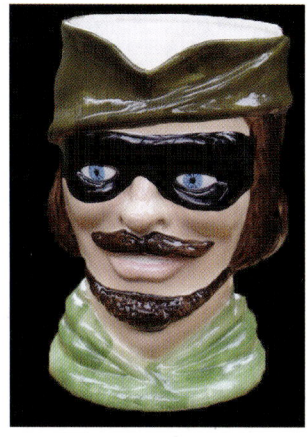

A faithful replica of the Toby Jug in the *Twelve O'clock High* movie.

Harvey Stovall turns the famous Toby Jug around to indicate that a mission is to be flown on the morrow.

There will be a briefing for a practice mission at 1100 this morning. That's right, practice. I've been sent here to take over what has come to be known as a hard luck group. Well, I don't believe in hard luck. So we're going to find out what the trouble is. Maybe part of it's your flying, so we're going back to fundamentals. But I can tell you now one reason I think you've been having hard luck. I saw it in your faces last night. I can see it there now. You've been looking at a lot of air lately… and you think you ought to have a rest. In short, you're sorry for yourselves. I don't have a lot of patience with this, 'What are we fighting for?' stuff. We're in a war, a shooting war. We've got to fight. And some of us have got to die. I'm not trying to tell you not to be afraid. Fear is normal. But stop worrying about it and about yourselves. Stop making plans. Forget about going home. Consider yourselves already dead. Once you accept that idea, it won't be so tough.

Now if any man here can't buy that… if he rates himself as something special, with a special kind of hide to be saved… he'd better make up his mind about it right now. Because I don't want him in this group.

I'll be in my office in five minutes. You can see me there.

General Frank Savage addressing the
918th for the first time at 0800 hours.

You're all going to die!

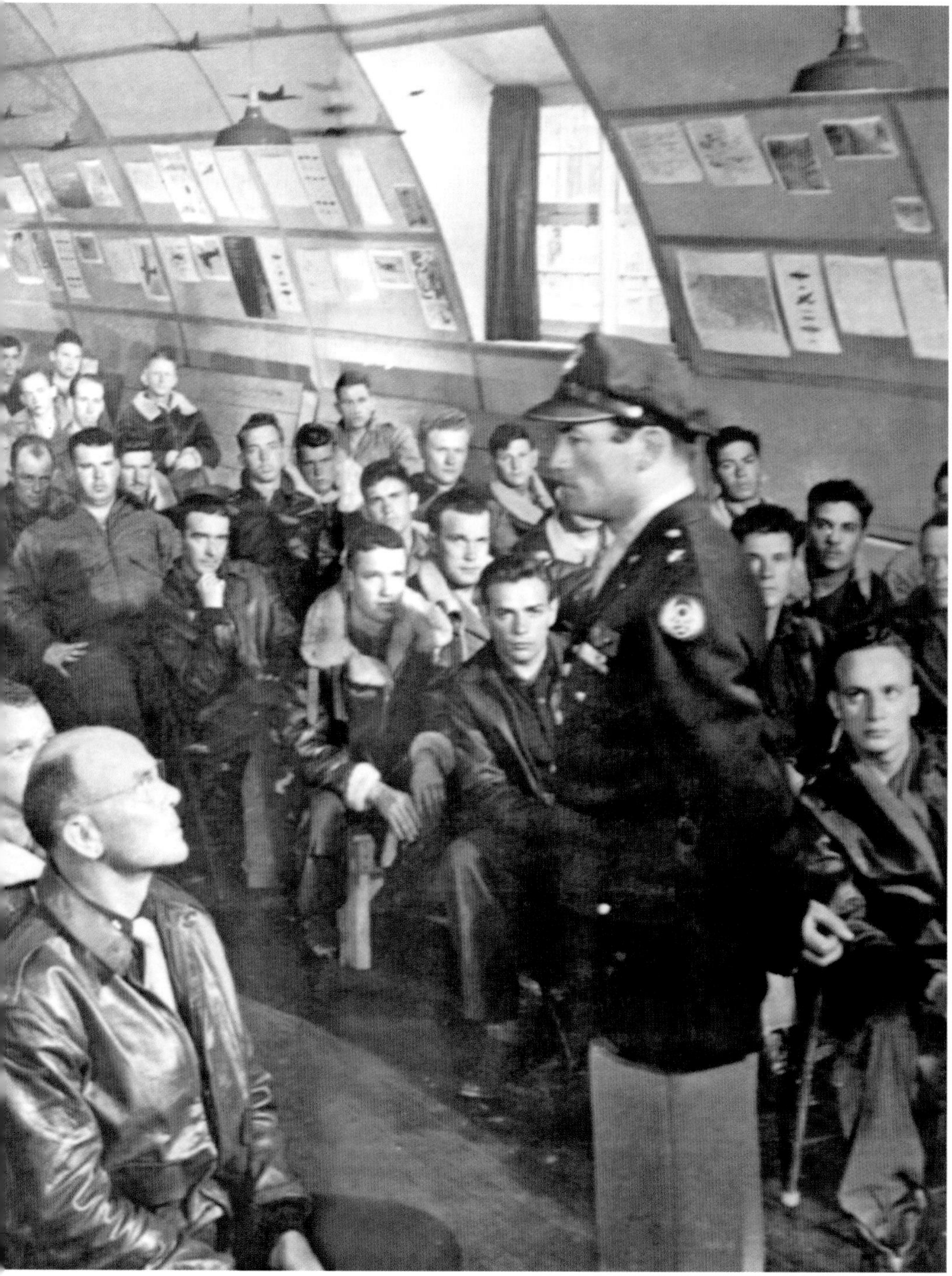

Movie poster of a mission briefing scene with 'General Savage' (Gregory Peck), 'Major General Patrick Pritchard' and (2nd from left) likeable, decent, 'Colonel Keith Davenport', played by Gary Merrill the outgoing 918th Bomb Group Commander.

'Lieutenant Colonel Ben Gately' played by Gary Marlow is 'chewed out' and demoted by General Savage after shirking responsibility and going AWOL. Savage orders Gately to paint the name *Leper Colony* on his B-17 and assigns him only misfits, backsliders and men known to be 'combat fatigued' or, as it was known, 'flak happy'. It is Gately's chance to get back his self-respect and become the heroic figure Savage knows deep down that he is.

Savage knows that wallowing in self-pity and calling themselves the 'Hard Luck Group' is not going to help the air crews, least of all place bombs squarely on target, the reason for their entire being. In what is arguably the most memorable scene in the movie, in the briefing room Savage finally brings the crews to the reality of their situation with swift, sharp, shock treatment. He stuns his new charges (and the audience) with a well-directed bucket of ice-cold water more accurate than a bomb strike. It chills every spine in the room and in every theatre across the country. Savage fires from the hip and tells them straight. The impact on the pale young faces has clearly found its mark. It is one of shell-shock, much more powerful than a burst of flak, or a salvo of machine gun fire in the cockpit.

In the persona of Frank Savage we witness his steady mental decline as battle fatigue overtakes and finally engulfs this remarkable leader of men. Ultimately, Savage allows the full weight of responsibility to fall squarely on his shoulders, and his alone, much in the same way that events had overtaken Davenport. Savage continues to fly missions when it is not essential or required of him to do so. He insists on leading from the front as if he still has something to prove to his men, He begins to crack and then suffers the final painful mental breakdown at planeside prior to a mission. He is so wracked with mental fatigue that he cannot summon strength in his arms to lift himself up and into the nose of his B-17. Although Lay largely modelled 'Savage' on Brigadier General Frank A. Armstrong, he was not the inspiration for this scene. This incident, as Lay confirmed, did happen to 'a very fine commander,' in all probability, Brigadier General Newton Longfellow, one of Eaker's closest friends since they had served in the Philippines in 1919. At the end of July 1942 Colonel Longfellow was put forward by Eaker for promotion to brigadier general. On 21 August Eaker placed Longfellow in command of the 1st Bomb Wing. On 24 August, seven days after the inaugural VIIIth Bomber Command mission to Rouen. Longfellow was aboard Major Paul Tibbets' B-17 (Armstrong's pilot on the momentous Rouen raid when he led a dozen 97th Bomb Group B-17s to Le Trait). It was the new bomb wing commander's combat orientation flight.

On the way home the formation was jumped from above by yellow-nosed Bf 109s which, during an overhead pass, fired 20mm cannon shells into Tibbets' cockpit, shattering the instrument panel and severely injuring the co-pilot, in the left hand. The top turret gunner was also seriously injured. Tibbets, who was also wounded, wrote

General Savage is led away from his plane after the pressure of commanding his group finally results in his complete mental breakdown.

Major (later General) Paul Tibbets of Miami, Florida, the 27-year-old Group Flying Executive Officer in the 97th Bomb Group who flew the first B-17 mission on 17 August 1942. In August 1945 he piloted the B-29, Enola Gay on the atomic-bomb-dropping mission on Hiroshima, Japan.

'I guess I don't have to tell you what's coming, Frank. I'm promising you nothing except a job no man should have to do who's already had more than his share of combat. I've gotta ask you to take nice kids and fly them until they can't take any more, and then put 'em back in and fly 'em some more. We've got to try to find out just what a maximum effort is. How much a man can take and get it all.' (General Pritchard [Millard Mitchell] in a tense scene in *Twelve O'clock High*).

later; 'Newt panicked. He started grabbing for the throttles and we had a critical situation. I told him to quit. He didn't even hear me. The only thing I could do was hit him with my right elbow. I was able to catch him under the chin, while he was leaning over and I knocked him flat on his fanny. He calmed down then and when he got back on his feet he spent the next half-hour ministering to the injured [and then] took over the co-pilot's duties to help me fly the plane.'

Longfellow was, according to Geoffrey Perret in his book *Winged Victory*; 'Perpetually overwrought, (he) struggled to overcome its (VIIIth Bomber Command's) difficulties by shouting himself hoarse... (His) nonstop ranting had earned him the nickname "Screaming Eagle." At the end of June (1943) he was sent home, a burned out wreck.'

Eaker recommended Longfellow to the commander of Second Air Force, a training command in the US, adding. 'He is a tireless worker and despite the fact that we almost killed him off here working, or carrying the responsibility, for 24 hours a day, seven days a week, I believe he will spring back after a few weeks' rest and do a tremendous job...' Longfellow got the job but was reduced to his regular rank as colonel.

Twelve O'clock High remains the classic US aviation movie of all time. Often seen on TV around the world, it also continues to be used for both military and managerial leadership courses as a training film for officer cadets and equally, for captains of industry. Beirne Lay, who also adapted his story for the TV series of the same name, died on 26 May 1982.

General Newton L. Longfellow, whose persona was most probably used to underwrite the complete mental breakdown scene in *Twelve O'clock High*.

Twelve O' clock High *was finally complete on 1 July 1949 and was premiered at Grauman's Chinese Theatre in Hollywood on Christmas Day 1949. Twenty-five years' later Gregory Peck summed up the movie perfectly when he said:* 'it is gratifying to be part of a movie that is still being shown 26 years after we made it. I think the picture still has meaning for audiences because of the integrity. We managed to dramatise a true story, without resorting to false theatrics and sentimentality.'

4. MOVIE STARS: MYTHS IN THE MISTS OF TIME

'I'm sure you saw it in Memphis Belle. *It's just a puff of black smoke. You see thousands ahead of you and fly right thru them. The more you see, naturally, the more worried you are (if you have sense enough to worry). But the ones you the see will never hurt you. You'll never see the one that rips into your wing or your engines or fuselage. Or possibly into one of your crew... I'm very glad that you saw the* Memphis Belle. *That is the most accurate picture of what we do that could possibly be shown. But believe me every mission isn't that bad. Still ships are lost and the only 'good' mission, to me, hasn't been flown since I've been here. That will be the one when none go down and no one is killed. It's mostly up to us. I read somewhere that those who fly in combat take their jobs much like steeple-jacks and coal miners. If you know it thoroughly and fully realize the disaster of being careless, or not being alert, then you don't worry. You get the feeling that it's up to you....'*

'Bill' Ligon in the 548th Bomb Squadron, 385th Bomb Group, at Great Ashfield, Suffolk. 'Bill' was KIA on 6 October 1944 on *Dozy Doats*, one of eleven Fortresses in the Group that were shot down on this costly raid.

The Belle

While the 306th Bomb Group unfortunately earned the epithet of being an 'unlucky group' and in later years the basis of a novel and a thought-provoking movie, at Bassingbourn the adventures of a B-17 sublimely called *Memphis Belle* engendered an entirely different movie, one that became a significant morale boost for its crew and the aircraft throughout the world when it appeared in cinemas in 1944. In America stirring deeds of the fine young men filled the newspapers and magazines of the period. They were crystallized in the minds of the population with movies such as William Wyler's wartime epic *Memphis Belle*, a poignant feature screened on both sides of the Atlantic, about the lives of a B-17 crew who ostensibly were the first in the Eighth Air Force to complete their tour of 25 missions over enemy targets.

During crew training at Walla Walla, Washington 'Bob' Morgan, pilot of the *Memphis Belle*, not yet a 1st Lieutenant began romancing Margaret Polk, of Memphis, Tennessee who was visiting her sister in Walla Walla. Legend has it that Margaret inspired the name *Memphis Belle*, which Morgan had painted on both sides of the fuselage of his B-17 at Bangor, Maine in September 1942 before leaving for Bassingbourn, an ex-RAF bomber station just north of Royston in Cambridgeshire. However, Morgan's co-pilot, Jim Verinis, recalled that he and Morgan went to see the movie *Lady For A Night* starring Joan Blondell and John Wayne. In the movie there is a Mississippi River gambling boat and Verinis remembered that either Miss Blondell or the boat was called the *Memphis Belle*. The romance between Morgan and the Memphis girl would flourish for

'Bob' Morgan (rear centre in cap) with his jubilant crew in front of the *Memphis Belle*.

William Wyler's daughter Catherine poses for my camera at Duxford during filming of the remake of *The Memphis Belle* which was released in 1990 to mixed reviews, one calling it 'a clichéd commercial production'. Any crew like the one portrayed who hated each other so much and never bonded in the air would not have survived one mission let alone 25. Probably the worst faux pas was the celebration scene for the crew's 25th and final mission – the night before they had even taken off!

a time and in England Morgan flew over the French sub pens and German dockyards in a sweater knitted by Margaret. A Hollywood scriptwriter would have had them married but war was no respecter of tradition and Morgan and Margaret later married other partners. The legendary artwork, though, remained indelibly painted on the nose of the B-17 through thick and thin.

Contrary to popular belief, *Memphis Belle* was not the first to complete an 8th Air Force tour (it was actually *Hell's Angels* in the 303rd Bomb Group at Molesworth) but then there would be no love story would there! The *Belle's* '25th mission' on 17 May 1943, to Lorient, was duly recorded using a 'stand-in' B-17F. The 16mm colour footage of the Belle's career in the ETO was used with great effect in the documentary. Everyone it seemed wanted to meet the famous men of the *Memphis Belle*. On 26 May they were introduced to HM King George VI and Queen Elizabeth at Bassingbourn and on 9 June General Eaker paid them a visit and then bade

The left side of the nose of the 'Belle'. In WW2 Corporal Tony Starcer was responsible for the artwork for this and 126 other Fortresses at Bassingbourn. (Author)

The right fuselage side of the 'Belle'. (Author)

them a stateside farewell to take part in a bond tour of US cities. Hollywood would have written that the pilot and his first love would marry and fly off into the sunset like the *Memphis Belle* but when Morgan's tour was completed in December, he did marry, but not to Margaret Polk, his Memphis belle, but Dotty Johnson, a hometown girl he met on his war bond tour.

What finally emerged in April 1945 was a colourful and exciting 38-minute masterpiece which gave American cinemagoers a timely reminder of the grim reality of the war which was being fought at high altitude in the skies over Europe. By this time a tour of missions had risen to 35 and the chances of completing them were even more remote than they had been in 1942–3. Britons saw the film for the first time in the winter of 1944–45.

> *'The 91st?' he says. 'Isn't that where they sent ol' Clark Gable?'*
>
> *He squints his eyes, puckers his mouth and in a real bad imitation of Gable says, 'Frankly my dear, I don't give a damn...'*
>
> **A Real Good War** by Sam Halpert.

'Jimmy' Stewart and Clark Gable take a break from the war.

'During briefing, a large groan erupted when the map of our mission was uncovered and we saw a long red ribbon heading straight to Berlin!' wrote Hank Wentland, a pilot in the 564th Squadron at Hethel, recalling the mission to Zossen on 13 March 1945. 'Our concerns were not assuaged when informed that we were not really going to Berlin but to a small town twenty miles south of "Big B". Wow, hope the Germans understand this! In closing we were told our Command Pilot for this mission would be Lieutenant Colonel "Jimmy" Stewart, who was in the back of the room. We turned and saw him, a tall, lean figure, nonchalantly leaning against the doorjamb. Oh, we caught the wrath of every 88mm battery on the way in. And before we reached the Initial Point Stewart came on the radio and said, *"OK f-f-fellas…let's pull it in real t-t-tight!"* Having heard the actor Jimmy Stewart stutter occasionally in pictures, I thought it was a cute affectation and now realized he had a real little verbal glitch. Anyhow, the German Officer Training groups in Zossen that were housed in tents, didn't enjoy their reveille call that morning consisting of 250lb bombs raining down and through their housing facilities.'

In July 1944 James Maitland Stewart, better known as 'Jimmy', was coming to the end of a very distinguished Liberator flying career. Everywhere the Hollywood actor went he was recognized, although on duty in the air and on the ground he was treated like any other officer – almost. In 1941, to everyone's amazement, he gave up his $16,000 (£3,250) a month salary in the movie industry and at 32 years of age, tried to enlist in the Army Air Corps. Stewart reported to Moffett Field, California on 21 March where he completed his basic training. By November 1943 Captain Stewart was Operations Officer of the 703rd Bomb Squadron in the 445th Bomb Group at Tibenham, Norfolk.

The 8th Air Force already boasted another Hollywood movie star, a rugged and handsome actor named Clark Gable, whose third wife Carole Lombard had died in an airplane crash. Emotionally and physically devastated, he decided to join the Army Air Force. Although he was beyond the draft age at the time the US entered the war, Gable enlisted as a private in the Army Air Force on 12 August 1942, attended the Officers' Candidate School at Miami Beach, Florida and graduated as a second lieutenant on in October. He then attended aerial gunnery school and in February 1943, on personal orders from General 'Hap' Arnold, went to England to make a motion picture about aerial gunners in action. He was assigned to the 351st Bomb Group at Polebrook. Although neither ordered nor expected to do so, he flew a few operational missions over Europe in B-17s to obtain the combat film footage he believed was required for producing the movie, titled *Combat America*.

Gable returned to the US in October 1943 and was relieved from active duty as a major on 12 June 1944, at his own request, since he was over-age for combat. Because his motion picture production schedule made it impossible for him to fulfil his AAF Reserve officer duties, he resigned his commission on 26 September 1947.

On 20 January 1944 James Stewart was promoted to major, a rank he had previously refused to accept until, as he said, 'My junior officers get promoted from lieutenants' and he took command of the 703rd Bomb Squadron. Next day he led the 445th Bomb Group to Bonnier, France and the 2nd Combat Wing to Frankfurt on the 29th. While at Tibenham a troubled Stewart wrote: 'Our group had suffered heavy casualties during the day. As the big ships settled in for landings, wings and fuselages bore ragged holes from fighter attack and antiaircraft fire. Bright red flares soared from planes carrying wounded, and ambulances raced to meet them.

'Men on the ground anxiously counted our squadron's incoming planes…nine…ten…eleven…then only an empty, grey sky. Where was the twelfth? Worried eyes swept the misty horizon, straining for some tiny dot, as hearts hoped against hope. But crewmembers in the returning planes knew that the missing ship would never land here again; German fighters had shot it down in flames.'

On 22 March Stewart led the wing again, this time to Berlin. This was his first trip to 'Big-B' and, when asked by newsmen if it was any more unusual than his others, Stewart said, 'Unusual? We hit Berlin, didn't we?'

By now the Top Brass considered that Stewart had been flying too many missions and he was moved on 30 March to the 453rd Bomb Group at Old Buckenham, Norfolk as Operations Officer to replace Major Curtis H. Cofield who had been killed in action only three days before. Over the next few weeks Stewart took his turn as Air Commander of bombing missions. On 13 April he flew 2nd Combat Wing lead against German aircraft manufacturing installations near Munich. All but one of the 453rd Bomb Group Liberators returned to Old Buckenham.

> *A Wonderful Life*
> 'One briefing I recall was conducted by Colonel James Stewart, who was then Group Operations Officer. He enlivened the proceedings with his dry wit and acting ability.'
>
> Frank J. 'Doc' Pickett MD, medical officer at Old Buckenham, Norfolk from 19 April 1944.

B-24 Liberator *Whiskey Jingles* in the 453rd Bomb Group at Old Buckenham in the winter of 1944 when it was flown on the 'Whiskey Run' to Scotland by 'Jimmy' Stewart.

Sergeant Melvin Borne, a ground crewman in the 733rd Squadron, flew with Stewart on many occasions when he piloted *Whiskey Jingles*. 'The biggest thrill of my life was the day he let me fly *Whiskey Jingles* back from Scotland to "Old Buck". We went there to get some whiskey. After one mission, when Jimmy Stewart led the wing in *Whiskey Jingles*, he taxied into the hardstand. I checked how much fuel showed on the sight gauges on the flight deck. I could only get the bottom of the dip stick wet and told Colonel Stewart, "Sir, you taxied in on fumes." Two days later Stewart led another mission. That night they made it home with about fifty gallons left.'

The wiry, highly-strung Stewart was now 36 years of age and his combat career was coming to an end. People in high places rightly considered him too valuable to lose and the decision was taken that he would fly no more missions. On 3 June 1944 Stewart was promoted to lieutenant colonel and on 1 July he moved to 2nd Combat Wing Headquarters at Hethel as chief of staff to Brigadier General Ted Timberlake. By the end of the war Stewart had completed 57 months active duty including 22 of them spent in the ETO (European Theater of Operations).

James Stewart died in June 1997 aged 89.

B-24 Liberators (one with its H_2X radome extended) in the 93rd 'Travelling Circus' Bomb Group from Hardwick.

American singer Irene Manning joins Major Glenn Miller for 'Music for the Wehrmacht' propaganda broadcast by the American Broadcasting Station In Europe (ABSIE) in London in November 1944. ABSIE was controlled by the Overseas Branch of the Office of War Information, a civilian propaganda outlet for the American Government.
(US Army)

The Real Glenn Miller Story?

Detective work has formed 90 percent of my research over the past forty years and if nothing else I have learned that 'history is not an exact science – it is an agreed upon lie'. According to Dr. James E. Crisp, North Carolina State University, *In history you don't ever get positive, conclusive evidence*'. He was referring to the death of Davy Crockett at the Alamo, which contrary to popular folklore, makes the claim that the American hero could in fact have committed suicide.

Speaking of legends, John Ford the famous Hollywood motion picture director (and incidentally, wartime OSS naval officer) once said that, *'When the legend becomes fact, print the legend.'*

The disappearance of Glenn Miller aboard a Norseman aircraft in the English Channel on 15 December 1944 has attracted widespread interest ever since the MIA (Missing In Action) was published shortly after the events of that fateful time but there is no mention in the control tower log for Alconbury/Abbots Ripton (where the flight originated) of a Norseman taking off or landing on the 15th; nor in the Operations Record Book (ORB) for Twinwood (where it reportedly picked up Miller en route for France) which says simply, 'there was no flying today'. So there might be a question mark about the flight and the events that followed.

> '*I was never able to understand the significance given to Twinwood airfield. The only evidence we have that G.M. took off from there on 15 December 1944 is the word of Don Haynes. That word is uncorroborated and it is known that several versions of Haynes' written statements exist. It is known that Haynes' statements about that event contain untruths. Therefore how do we know what is really true and what is false? We don't! I see no value of studying detailed facts about the physics of that location. It is really not relevant.*'
>
> **Gordon Lee 'Tex' Beneke, American saxophonist, singer and bandleader who joined the Glenn Miller Orchestra in 1938. When the Miller estate authorized an official Glenn Miller 'ghost band' in 1946, it was led by 'Tex' Beneke. Don Haynes was Glenn Miller's Executive Officer whose diary entries have been widely used to try to explain the events leading up to Miller's disappearance.**

One can only speculate further.

5. CASTLES IN THE AIR

Only death in a cold, cold grave
for that brave crew their lives they gave
Instead of dying in that infernal machine
they should have lived to glory in a B-17

'BOMBER station in England, June 28, 1943 – The days are very long. A combination of summer time and daylight-saving time keeps them light until eleven-thirty. After mess we take the Army bus into town. It is an ancient little city which every American knows about as soon as he can read. The buildings on the narrow streets are Tudor, Stuart, Georgian, and even some Norman. The paving stones are worn smooth and the flagstones of the sidewalks are grooved by ages of strollers. It is a town to stroll in. American soldiers, Canadians, Royal Air Force men and many of Great Britain's women soldiers walk through the streets and Britain drafts its women and they are really in the Army, driver-mechanics, dispatch riders, trim and hard in their uniforms.

'The crew of the *Mary Ruth* ends up at a little pub, over-crowded and noisy. They edge their way in to the bar, where the barmaids are drawing beer as fast as they can. In a moment this crew hits found a table and they have the small glasses of pale yellow fluid in front of them. It is curious beer. Most of the alcohol has been taken out of it to make munitions. It is not cold. It is token beer – a gesture rather than a drink.

'The bomber crew is solemn. Men who are alerted for operational missions are usually solemn, but tonight there is some burden on this crew. There is no way of knowing how these things start. All at once a crew will feel fated. Then little things go wrong. Then they are uneasy until they take off for their mission. When the uneasiness is running it is the waiting that hurts.

'They sip the flat, tasteless beer. One of them says. "I saw a paper from home at the Red Cross in London." It is quiet. The others look at him across their glasses. A mixed group of pilots and ATS girls at the other end of the pub have started a song. It is astonishing how many of the songs are American. *"You'd Be So Nice to Come Home to,"* they sing. And, the beat of the song is subtly changed. It has become an English song.'

'They stand up and file slowly out of the pub. It is still daylight. The pigeons are flying about the tower of an old Gothic church, a kind of architecture especially suited to nesting pigeons.

'The hotel taken over by the Red Cross is crowded with men in from the flying fields which dot the countryside. Our bus drives up in front and we pile in. The crew looks automatically at the sky. It is clear, with little puffs of white cloud suspended in the light of a sun that has already gone down.

"Looks like it might be a clear day," the radio man says.

"That's good for us and it's good for them to get at us."

'The bus rattles back toward the field. The tail gunner muses. "I hope old Red Beard (an enemy fighter pilot who comes so close that you can almost see his face) has got a bad cold," he says.

"I didn't like the look in his eye last time."'

Once There Was A War by John Steinbeck (1943)

Day-dreaming and building castles in the air can sometimes also be inspiring. (Ross Greening)

First Lieutenant Loren E. Roll and Mary Ruth King on their wedding day on Friday, 19 March 1943 – one week after they met! The crew decided to name the plane *Mary Ruth – Memories of Mobile* in honour of Loren's new wife. The serial number of the Fortress was Mary Ruth King's phone number in Mobile at the time she met Loren!

'Mary Ruth' Memories of Mobile in the 91st Bomb Group at Bassingbourn and Lieutenant Kenneth L. Brown and crew's visit to Cambridge nearby is the subject of this wartime censored story. In February 1943 1st Lieutenant Loren Roll and crew were sent to Salinas, Kansas to pick up a new B-17 to ferry it to England by way of South America and North Africa. They got as far as West Palm Beach, Florida when they discovered the engines were using too much oil. It was learned the oil rings in the pistons had been inserted upside down. They were sent back to the major aircraft repair centre at Brookley Field in Mobile, Alabama to have the engines replaced, which was quicker than replacing the rings. The crew stayed at the Battlehouse Hotel in downtown Mobile, where, on Friday, March 12th Loren and another crew member were having a drink in the hotel lounge and started talking to the two women sitting at the next table. Mary Ruth King and her friend did sheet-metal work repairing planes at Brookley Field. Loren and Mary Ruth hit it off immediately. They went out every evening the next week, except for a couple of nights when Mary Ruth had to work the swing shift. They spent hours and hours talking, since there was not much to do for entertainment during the war. Loren proposed after a few days and they were married at Dauphin Way Baptist Church on 19 March – one week after they met! The crew decided to name the plane *Mary Ruth – Memories of Mobile* in honor of Loren's new wife.

Loren and his crew were assigned to a replacement pool at the 92nd Bomb Group. Two were shot down, but survived the war. The others successfully completed their missions and returned to the States; Loren flew 31 combat missions.

On 22 June 1943 *'Mary Ruth'* was being flown by Lieutenant Kenneth L. Brown and crew when it failed to return. Two of the crew were killed; eight survived and were taken into captivity.

B-17 42-29536 *Mary Ruth – Memories of Mobile* in the 91st Bomb Group at Bassingbourn.

View into the astrodome. (Author)

Co-Pilot 2nd Lieutenant F. N. Dibble of Bronxville, NY and 1st Lieutenant James M. 'Smitty' Smith of Austin, Texas at the controls of *Our Gang* just before take-off on another bombing mission over enemy territory in June 1943.

1st Lieutenant James M. 'Smitty' Smith with 'Skippy' a cocker spaniel which was probably one of the most pampered mascots at Bassingbourn. Both had over 200 hours flying time when this photo was taken in April 1943. The crew had two canine mascots: 'Windy' and 'Skipper', from Casper, Wyoming.

'Our Gang'

'The scene is a Fortress field. Even in the early fog light of English dawn, you could tell that this Foil had a new wing. And on her nose there was a familiar name: *Our Gang*. Remember what happened to the old wing? That was the one that got chewed up at Hüls weeks ago. This was the dawning of August 17, first birthday of the brazen, bloody daylight storming of Hitler's Fortress Europe by the Flying Forts of the US Eighth Air Force.'

August the 17th 1943 was to be a rugged day; the Field Order called for ambitious and daring strikes on the aircraft plant at Regensburg and the ball-bearing plant at Schweinfurt.

Captain John R. 'Tex' McCrary, war reporter for 8th Air Force Public Relations, a Texan, who had once worked on the New York *Mirror*, which always specialized in 'Rape, riot and ruin', was no desk bound war reporter. When he wanted to hitch a ride aboard a Flying Fortress he normally headed for Bassingbourn. The Cambridgeshire base became famous for drawing press and photographers from London to its portals like a siren. It was more easily accessible from London than most bases in far-flung East Anglia with its poor road and rail links. It was the station that McCrary had done most of his 'hitch-hiking' as he called it, flying three missions with Captain Oscar O'Neill's crew and he had 'got to know them pretty well'. McCrary had flown the 23 June mission to Hüls in *'Our Gang'* flown by 'Smitty' Smith. 'Tex' had been so sure that the raid would be scrubbed and his initial nervousness had ebbed away but the raid had gone ahead and he flew the mission in Smith's ship. As fate would have it McCrary was down to fly the Schweinfurt raid aboard Harry Lay's ship *Bad Egg*, but this was changed just before take-off to *'Our Gang'*, which this time was being piloted by Bill Wheeler from Scarsdale, New York.

'Tex' McCrary was 'scared as hell' when he pulled up inside the nose of *'Our Gang'* to tell Wheeler that he was carrying a hitch-hiker. Fear had been piling up in the coils of McCrary's guts for days. He knew that this job would rank with the first raid on Berlin and the first night raid in drama, excitement and importance. He wanted to be a ringside and he wanted to find out if he could 'cure' fear. McCrary found that he couldn't.

> *Luck is No Lady* by Captain John R. ('Tex') McCrary. The Texan reporter did not know whether or not it was the crew or the ship or him that 'had run out of luck' but McCrary knew that *'Our Gang'* would not get home. He went out to the Fortress, invented a lame story about being 'sure that they're going to scrub it', collected his cameras and flying clothes out of the nose and drove on back to the officers' club. In all, sixty Fortresses were lost on 17 August. Enemy fighters KO'd the #1 and #2 engines and *'Our Gang'* lagged behind before crashing at St. Goar, 15 miles south of Coblenz, Germany. All ten crew bailed out safely. See *First of the Many* by Captain John R. (Tex) McCrary and David E. Scherman (1944).

'The briefing room buzzed as each man tried to divine his fate in chalk marks much as prophets used to study the flight of geese or the entrails of slaughtered sheep. Is a high spot in the formation good or bad? Is it true that Jerry is picking on the high ones, as the fellow said at mess? Or did he say it was the low groups that were getting it? I quite forgot the meaning of the augury.

'The colonel held up his hand to stop the speculation.

"Gentlemen", he said in a tone which had a solemn ring for all its casualness, "we've come this far to do a job. Let's do a good one. That's all." It was crisp and brassy West Point.

'The pilots shambled to their feet and filed out. The bombardiers queued for their target charts. The navigators flocked to another room where Dutch, the group navigator, was sitting cross-legged on a rickety table, reading aloud his computations of headings, winds, ground speeds and airspeeds in a prayer-like drone. At his side lay a stack of flimsies summarizing the data. I took a few notes, picked up a flight plan and admired my set of gorgeous linen maps in aquamarines and blues and browns.'

Elmer Bendiner, B-17 rear gunner,
379th Bomb Group, Alconbury.

Bomb sight in a B-17. (Author)

Formation of B-17G Flying Fortresses in the 447th Bomb Group at Rattlesden over England.

'We roam through fields in the long summer sunlight, coming across B-17s in their dispersal areas close to barns, sheds and farm houses. Just about every plane we see, the old olive drab painted ships as well as the newer, shiny unpainted jobs, is spotted with pieces of sheet metal riveted on like patches on a vaudeville tramp's coat. A piece of bright aluminium about four feet square is outlined against the olive drab right wing of Round Trip II... "Oh man that ship has seen some action."'

A Real Good War by Sam Halpert.

The late lamented *Liberty Belle* in close formation with the *Memphis Belle* movie stand-in owned by the Liberty Foundation in Claremore, Oklahoma, on loan from the Military Aircraft Restoration Corporation in Anaheim, California. The name *Liberty Belle* was popular with over two dozen known individual Flying Fortresses and Liberators using the name in combat in World War II. (Author)

P-51 Mustang *The Iowa Beaut* flown by Lieutenant Robert Hulderman in the 355th Fighter Group maintains formation while escorting B-17s in the 381st Bomb Group at Ridgewell.

'Goldie'

'Our twenty-five missions were not simple, each one worse that the last, but when we were briefed on 4 March 1944 for our twenty-fifth and last we had hoped for an easy run and then home to the good old USA but that was not to be the case. The target this day was to the first daylight raid on Berlin. It was the worst possible news that the *"Worry Wart"* crew could hear. We went through our pre-flight ritual as we always did, but this one had a special meaning. All went routinely until we were well into the flight, suddenly the entire force was recalled, the best possible news that I could hear over my radio. The fact that we were going home was sweet music to our crew when I told them of the recall, but someone said, can we take our bombs home on our last mission, we all said no, let us unload on any target. We voted unanimously to do so. We dropped back out of formation away from the protection of our fellow bomb group, probably the dumbest thing that we could do because any enemy fighter pilot that saw a lone bomber immediately saw this as a kill and that is exactly what happened. We unloaded our bombs on a railroad yard and began our climb back to the formation, which now were miles ahead of us when suddenly there was a loud explosion and immediately we dove for the cloud cover below us. This quick action by our pilots probably saved our plane and us from destruction. When we checked in by position, no one was hurt and we saw no battle damage. Every time we left the cloud cover there were more enemy fire at us, but we managed to escape. When "BJ" asked me for a radio position report from the RAF rescue station I was not sure I could handle it, but through German jamming of the message I was able to receive the position report, passed it on to our navigator and he plotted a course for England. When we came out of the clouds over the English Channel and saw the White Cliffs of Dover it was the most beautiful sight that I could ever hope to see. At this moment I did not realize the importance of my radio work, I had been too scared at that moment, but my training had paid off.

'Our landing at the base was not routine. We had no brakes and as we hit the runway we kept rolling until we left the end of the runway and came to an abrupt stop in a farmer's ploughed field. When the emergency vehicles reached us they wanted to know how bad the radio operator was hurt, but as I was standing there in one piece someone wondered why that question was asked. When the damage to the plane was pointed out to us we realized how lucky we were to be home safely. When a large hole in the radio room was pointed out to me, it was then that I knew I was fortunate not to be injured. The hole was where my head might have been but somehow I had ducked and lucky for me that I did. The next morning we all went out to the plane to look it over more closely, and when we saw the many holes and damage to the outer skin it was then that we all said our thanks in our own way. A few days later, "BJ" came into our quarters and ordered us all to accompany him to the base chapel and there we really became one crew that was thankful for our completing our missions without a major injury.'

Staff Sergeant Lawrence Goldstein, born in Brooklyn on 10 February 1922, radio operator on *The Worry Wart* crew in the 388th Bomb Group at Knettishall piloted by 'BJ' Keirsted.

Larry Goldstein wearing a WW2 flak suit. (Author)

The crew of *I'll Get By* take a ride in a jeep for a publicity photograph at Horham. This B-17 was lost in combat on 2 August 1944.

'Big-B'

'I wanted to be in on the March 4 Berlin mission and have the honour of being the first air commander to lead a raid over all three Axis capitals. I planned to fly a P-51 with one wingman ahead of the bomber stream over the capital city. To prepare for this, I sharpened up my fighter skills in the P-51 and then approached "Tooey" Spaatz to get his permission. I thought I might be able to persuade him to let me go, just as I had talked Hap Arnold into letting me lead the Tokyo Raid. "Tooey" finally gave in and reluctantly said I could go. However, just a day or so before our departure, "Tooey" changed his mind and said he couldn't afford to risk the capture of a senior officer who had knowledge of the invasion plans. So, contrary to what some have claimed for me, I did not participate in any bombing raids of Berlin. I admit, however, that I really wanted that honour.'

General 'Jimmy' Doolittle.

'Almost as quickly as it happened before the clouds once more closed up. On we flew, courageously, brave and scared as hell. We wondered if our P-51 escort knew that a small number of struggling B-17s were still heading for Berlin and whether the '51s would be at Berlin when we got there – or if the German Air Force fighters were waiting for us at Berlin, in which case it would be another Battle of Little Big Horn.'

Pathfinder bombardier Marshall Thixton,
482nd Bomb Group, Berlin raid, 4 March 1944.
Marshall Thixton was a bombardier who lived his early
life at the State Orphan's home in Corsicana, Texas.
Upon his graduation in 1941, Thixton left the home
with all his worldly possessions slung in a bag over his
shoulder and six dollars and fifty cents in his pocket.

Wilbur Richardson, who watched the 1,000 lb bomb go by his ball turret and saw it hit the left stabilizer of *Miss Donna Mae*, seen here reminiscing during an air show at Detroit in July 2007. Wilbur flew 30 missions in 79 days. Seriously wounded on the 30th over Munich on 13 July 1944, after five weeks in hospital he was offered the rank of Master Sergeant and leader of bomb storage dump. He turned it down because his brother was a casualty and Wilbur felt he should return. (Author)

During the Berlin mission of 19 May 1944 1,000 lb bombs falling from *Trudy* in the 94th Bomb Group severed the tailplane of *Miss Donna Mae* which went into an uncontrollable spin and at 13,000 feet part of the wing broke off, sending the Fortress crashing into the German capital and killing all eleven crew.

Kismet

On 19 May 1944 Lieutenant John Moser's crew in the 94th Bomb Group at Bury St Edmunds (Rougham) flew their first mission to Berlin. They had to abort their first scheduled run to the 'Big City' on 29 April. First, *Luscious Duchess* had developed turbo problems and then the second ship had a runaway prop at altitude. 2nd Lieutenant Kenneth L. Chisum's crew that took their place were shot down. Wilbur Richardson, Moser's ball turret gunner recalls: 'What made the 19 May trip memorable was that on the bomb run the ship above us [*Trudy*, flown by Lieutenant John Winslett] missed us with his bomb load. One of the 1,000-pounders fell behind No. 3 engine (I saw this one go by my ball turret). I quickly followed it down only to see it hit the left stabilizer of *Miss Donna Mae*, which was out of position below us. Apparently, it jammed the elevator in a down position. It lost attitude rapidly and began a steep dive. I watched in vain for 'chutes. None appeared. Others indicated that the Fort started to break up although I didn't see it. The flak was heavy and some fighters were in the area but Brüx had been much worse.'

On Thursday 13 July on the mission to Munich Wilbur Richardson flew his thirtieth and final mission of his tour, in *Kismet*.

All went well until 23,000 feet over Belgium, about 35 miles from Liège, his right outboard engine burst into flame and the propeller had to be feathered. The deputy lead ship took over and General Fred Castle dropped down to 20,000 feet. But at this height the aircraft began vibrating badly and he was forced to take it down another 3,000 feet before levelling out. The Fortress was now down to 180 mph indicated air speed and being pursued by seven Bf 109s. They attacked and wounded the tail gunner and left the radar navigator nursing bad wounds in his neck and shoulders. Castle could not carry out any evasive manoeuvres with the full bomb load still aboard and he could not salvo them for fear of hitting Allied troops on the ground. Successive attacks by the fighters put another two engines out of action and the B-17 lost altitude. To reduce airspeed the wheels of the Fortress were lowered and the crew ordered to bail out with the terse intercom message, *this is it boys*. Castle managed to level out; long enough for six of the crew to bail out but at 12,000 feet the bomber was hit in the right wing fuel tank, which exploded, sending the B-17 into a plunging final spiral to the ground. Castle was posthumously awarded the Medal of Honor; the highest ranking officer in the 8th AF to receive the award. Harriman and Castle were buried in the American cemetery at Henri-Chattel.

Lalli Coppinger, a Red Cross girl at Bury St Edmunds (Rougham) concludes that 'Great sorrow was felt throughout the base. As former Commander of the 94th, General Castle had earned the respect and affection of officers and enlisted men. He was known as a fearless pilot and a top leader. On his promotion day he had visited the unit and expressed his appreciation at all levels. The local English people who knew him remember him with great affection, because in their opinion he stood for every fine and decent thing about people, a credit to the United States, typifying the best in all Americans who came to England.' His loss was a great blow to the men who had come under his leadership.

'Thus ended Christmas 1944. A bright spot in the midst of the gloom was the many letters received by the 94th, praising them for the fine job they did as hosts to 70 or more diverted aircraft and their aircrews of 700 men and the help they provided at a time of peril.'

'The very thought of making a raid on Berlin was almost terrifying. Rumours began flying thick and fast several weeks before the day of the Berlin mission arrived, adding to the apprehension and anxiety. Each day we would walk into the briefing sessions wondering if the tape on the wall map would stretch to "Big-B" that morning. A great sigh of relief could be heard from the crews when the briefing officer pulled back the curtain and the tape went somewhere else.'

Captain Robert J. Shoens, pilot of *Our Gal' Sal'* in the 'Bloody Hundredth' Bomb Group at Thorpe Abbotts.

Lavenham

Lady Street and the 'Swan' in the picturesque village of Lavenham in Suffolk. (Author)

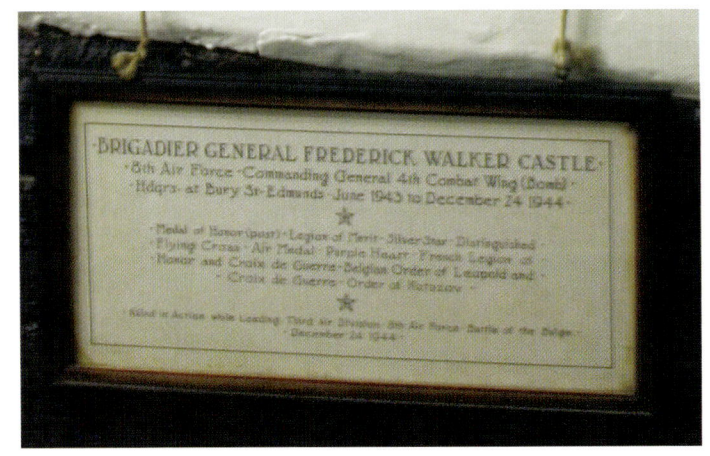

The portrait of General Fred Castle, commanding the 4th Bomb Wing who was KIA on the Christmas Eve raid on German targets in the Ardennes in 1944, which is displayed in the Swan Hotel at Lavenham.

51

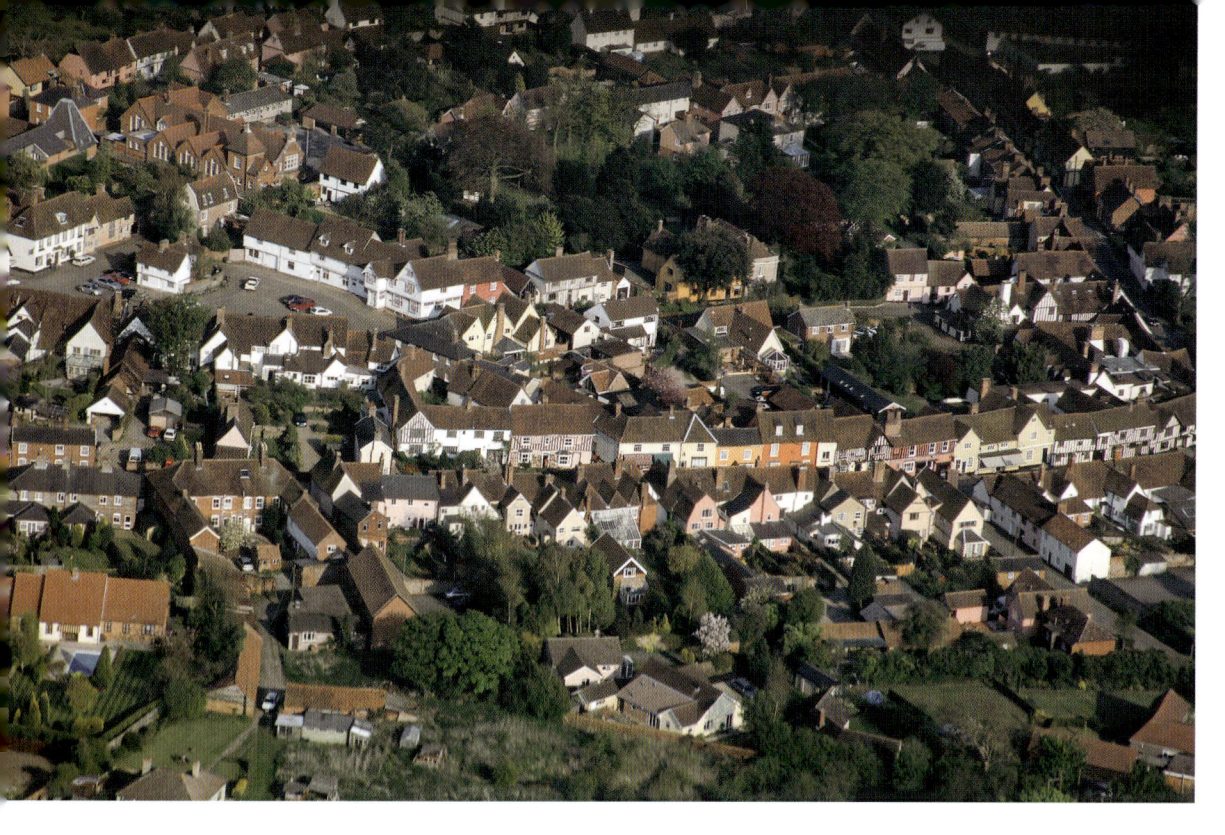

Aerial view of Lavenham
(Author)

Half-timbered houses in Lavenham.(Author)

Wartime signatures on a wall in the Swan at Lavenham.

6. CHRISTMAS IN THE ETO

'No one could ever forget those Christmas parties for the orphans and evacuee children, with the kids yelling and gobbling ice cream, sitting on our shoulders and singing for us.... going home along the lane clutching armfuls of toys and candy, chewing gum and biscuits. Fifteen hundred we had at one party.'

Left and right: 93rd Bomb Group Christmas card sent by Sergeant Colborn in the 93rd 'Travelling Circus' Bomb Group at Hardwick to Muriel, his English fiancée who was from Norwich, Norfolk.

> Merry Christmas Sweetheart. What a wonderful Christmas for me dear. Thank you honey. This is our first Christmas together. Wish I could have bought you a real nice present dear, one that you should have and sure wish I could have sent you a nicer card. Thanks for being so wonderful to me honey. Hope I can make you as happy as you've made me. Our next Christmas will be at home dear. I want you to be so happy. We have wonderful days

TED'S FLYING CIRCUS WISH YOU A MERRY CHRISTMAS — 2ND CHRISTMAS IN THE E.T.O.

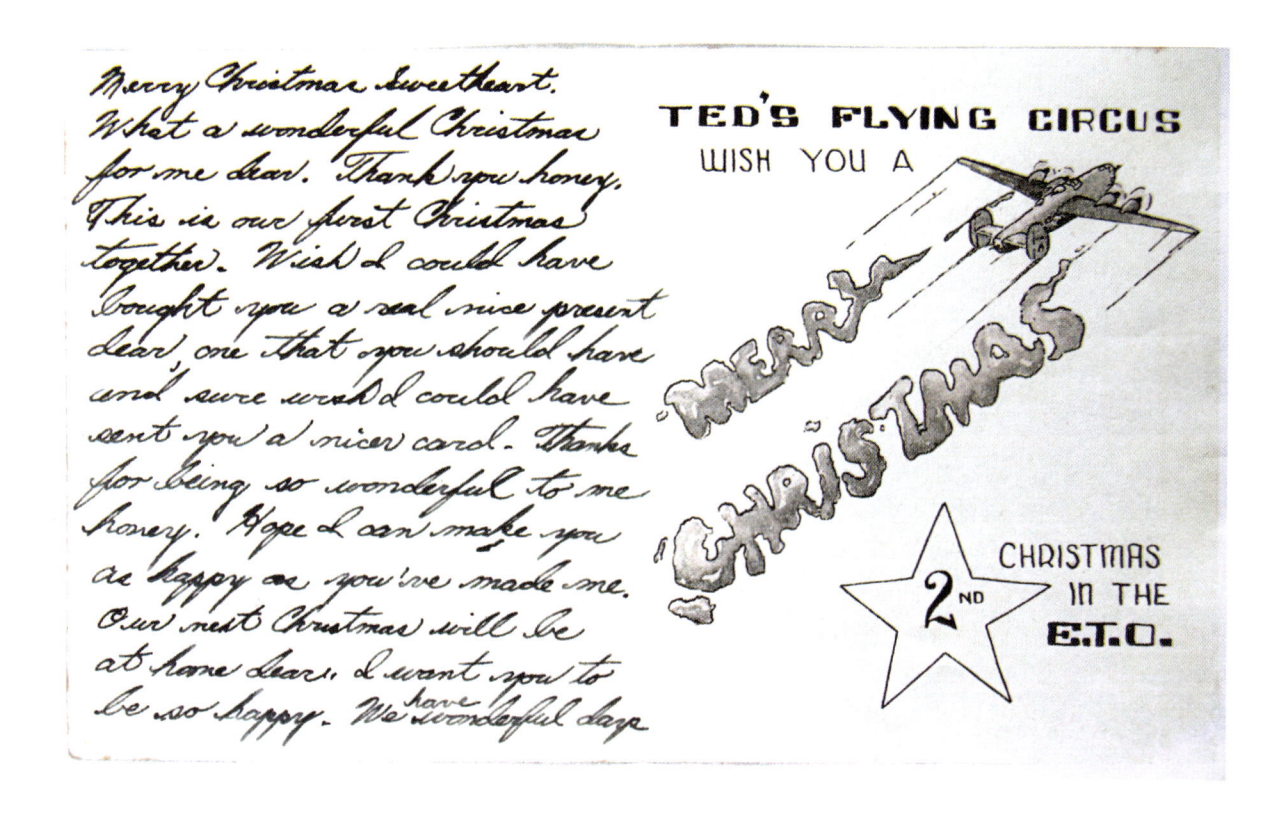

'I met my future wife at Christmas 1942. We had a few dates and then didn't have any dates, then had some more dates. We had to get permission to marry and I had to fight like hell, 'cause my commanding officer did not believe in marriage. He said, "Have as many common wives as you want, but don't sign no papers and get married." He did his best to talk guys out of it. I was persistent and I got a couple of other officers to talk for me, and finally he consented. We finally got the job done, Tuesday August the 15th 1944 at 2.30 pm at St Leonard's church in Bedford.'

**Technical Sergeant Walt Hagemeier Jr.,
a radio operator in the 306th Bomb Group**

A 'Flying Eightball' Christmas card originating from the 44th Bomb Group at Shipdham in Norfolk.

Sunday 13 August: 'had a chicken dinner when we got back today. Ice cream too…Things look better every day, don't they? I don't think it will last too much longer. In fact, a lot of fellas expect to be home for Christmas…'

William Y. 'Bill' Ligon Jr in the 548th Bomb Squadron, 385th Bomb Group, at Great Ashfield, Suffolk.

Local children at a party especially for them at Framlingham on 23 December 1943.

Entertaining local children at Deopham Green airbase near Norwich.

'From where we lived it was only a few hundred yards to Knettishall airfield and, I learned much later, the dispersal area of the 562nd Squadron of the 388th Bombardment Group. Many other local boys and I would visit the airfield often, at weekends and holidays, to get close to the Flying Fortresses parked there. The favourite cry was, "Got any gum, Chum?" whenever we met a GI.

'Other highlights were the Christmas parties given by the base for all the local schools. We were picked up from school in American trucks and taken to the base where we had film shows, a meal with more food than we had ever seen and a present off the tree from Santa Claus. I still have a book received at one of these parties, *Meetoo and the Little Creatures.*'

The 388th and Me – David Calcutt.

Children queue to see Santa at a Christmas party for the local children at Bassingbourn. It is all too much to take in for one girl at the left of the picture.

'…At Bury St. Edmunds 1,500 children swarmed the largest hall in town for an afternoon of riotous entertainment and at Ipswich there was a similar party for 1,100 more. At some airfields Santa Claus arrived from the sky in a Flying Fortress and at other camps they appeared in the inevitable jeep. At Kettering there was a special party for six children who had somehow been left out of the first party for seven hundred. At Hull there were plays and pantomimes at parties where each child was adopted by an American "pal", while at Bedford the American soldiers were "buddies", and at Colchester the military police entertained ninety children – all of them with fathers who were prisoners of war.

'There were stories in all the provincial newspapers that week, with headlines that read, "US Hosts to Northants Children", and "American Visitors Entertain More English Children", and "US Santa Claus Revisits Kettering", and "Yanks Play Santa Claus at Wellingborough", and "Thanks to the Yanks", But the truest one of all, I think, appeared in the *Rushden Echo and Argus* and it said "Americans Revel in Children's Visit". For that, in the end, was just about the way it was.'

The Children Of Britain, **Robert S. Arbib Jr.**

'Tex' and his buddies at tables with their young English guests. Americans were very good to the children and they were invited to the bases on special occasions at Thanksgiving and Christmas for a party. At long lunch tables, set for crowds of children, foil-wrapped chocolate bars laid end to end down the centre, pumpkin pie – a marvellous new taste – and turkey and cranberry sauce ('They put jam on their meat' one girl told her mother later) were new delights to British kids on the ration.

B-17G 44-8183/Q in the 418th Bomb Squadron, 100th Bomb Group in the snow at Thorpe Abbotts.

A Christmas party for British children at Kimbolton.

'My first recollections of the 8th Air Force were cycling a few miles to Deenethorpe airfield to watch the return of the 401st Bomb Group B-17s from their missions. Sometimes I noted the damaged planes as they came in to land. When two red flares were fired from an aircraft it signified that there were wounded aboard or perhaps something worse. Ambulances raced to the planes to attend to the injured as soon as they turned off the runway. Sadly, there were a few crashes near my home. Some were take-off crashes and some mid-air collisions with many fatalities among the crews. I visited a few of these crashes and it was a very sad sight to see. I always thought that it was some mother's son who had died so far from their homes. In December 1944 US trucks transported all the local school children (me included) to the base for a Christmas party. Bananas, ice cream, oranges and turkey were all on the menu. Quite a treat for us kids. We were each given a small toy made by the GIs to take home. Trucks then took us all safely home. How could I ever forget generous Yanks?'

Paul Knight.

'On Christmas Day at about 1400 hours a bunch of 6-bys trucks came along and we loaded up and were hauled back across England to our base at Kimbolton. We were served a really fine Christmas dinner in the mess hall at about 1800 hours, which made up for that long cold bouncy ride in that fine truck across England.'

Bill Brown, an armourer-gunner-togglier in the 379th Bomb Group.

'When the last planes were leaving the English coast the first groups were bombing Germany and we were one of the last planes, eating up all the prop wash in the sky that was just a sea of it. It was a short mission and should have been an easy one but the Jerries had guns all over the front and were throwing up very accurate flak at us all the way to the target and back. For the first time on a mission I had a completely visual run. After I had toggled the bombs I watched the target. Euskirchen was a small town and would never have been bombed at all if it weren't so close to the front. I saw red flashes spring up all over the town and thought that it was the muzzle flash of the flak guns until I saw black smoke roll out from each of the flashes and I realised that it was our bombs striking. Then while I watched Euskirchen was eradicated. What little of the town we hadn't hit was plastered by the squadron behind us. When we turned to the Rally Point there was nothing but smoke. At bombs away Bob Wallace looked down at Germany and hollered, "Merry Christmas you bastards".

'It couldn't have been too happy a one with 2,000 bombers dropping about 6,000lbs apiece all over a wide sector of Germany.'

Joe L. Nathan, navigator, 448th Bomb Group at Seething, Norfolk.

7. GHOST FIELDS OF LITTLE AMERICA

"I was alone in the tower in the ground floor front room at about 1.45 pm, paint brush in hand. A breeze came through the room, then noises started, aircraft engines and radios (RT) followed by men shouting. I was oblivious to anything else other than the noise, but five minutes before I had glanced out of the window and thought what a wonderful day it was.'
    The late Sam Hurry (a Diss schoolboy in WWII) during renovation of the tower at Thorpe Abbotts.

'A pilot was having problems completing his missions. He was convinced that if he stayed with his Squadron he would be killed so he asked his squadron commander to move him to another Group. He was told that if he moved, others would wish to follow so he had to stay. He was sent to a rest home for a week and reported back to his squadron commander and notified him he still wished to move. His request was refused and told that he was detailed for a mission next day. His bunkmate was a staff officer who worked in the control tower. He called in to see him and told him that if he was killed he would come back to haunt the tower. Next day over the target the pilot was killed.

'Many years after the war the chairman of a branch of the British Legion visited the tower, which was now a museum, to take photographs for his granddaughter, who was using the history of the airfield as part of her 'O level' exams. He came out of the tower in a hurry looking rather pale and told staff that he had seen a figure dressed in World War II American flying clothes. He was also unable to operate his camera. Others claim to have seen this ghostly figure.

'A gentleman from the North of England phoned to say he had an officer's hat given to his father who worked on the airfield during the war in return for some eggs. He was invited down and the hat was produced. The name in the hat was that of the officer who had requested a move from the group at the airfield.'

Anon

Starting of engines in the early morning, tannoy announcements and Morse and telephone conversations are just some of the sounds that are often still heard on deserted East Anglian air bases.

On operations I fly with ghostly air gunners
In the gun turret with me the ghosts ride
Eight times I've replaced ill-fated air gunners
Who in the turret where I now sit have died

I am sure that they are there to protect me
To save me from the grim fate that was theirs
Like wraiths appear their faces and bodies
Visions surrounding me in the gun turret airs

No other mortals have seen these ghost faces
Only I have gazed on their pale ghostly face
The faces of eight unfortunate air gunners
Who as squadron gunner I'd had to replace

Perhaps these ghostly gunners are an illusion
Maybe only in my imagination do they dwell
But in my judgement they are no apparition
I see the ghosts of eight gunners who fell

Air Gunner Ghosts, 9 October 1944 from
'No Place To Hide' by George 'Ole' Olson
RCAF during his tour of operations 1943-45

Sounds from primitive personnel accommodations like Nissen huts are often heard in the ether.

The Curse Of Tutankhamun? – A Norfolk Ghost Story

Based at Shipdham, Liberators of the 44th Bomb Group – the 'Flying Eightballs' – regularly assembled over Norfolk and joined the bomber fleets of the Second Air Division striking out across the North Sea for enemy occupied Europe. In tiny hamlets such as West Bradenham, close to Shipdham airbase, men on reserved occupation worked the fields around the Bradenham Hall estate, helping to provide desperately needed food for an embattled nation. Bradenham Hall is a two-storey Georgian house, set in several thousand acres of arable and fruit farmland, owned for a hundred years, from 1819–1919, by the Haggard family. Henry Haggard's great-grandson, Sir Henry Rider Haggard (of *King Solomon's Mines* fame) was born in 1856 at Wood Farm on what is now the Bradenham Estate. Bradenham Hall, with its fine garden and arboretum, sits near the top of one of Norfolk's highest hills, providing visitors with a splendid view to the south over rolling farmland. The garden and arboretum extend to around 27 acres and surround a fine early red brick Georgian house which has many local historical connections (Rider's dog 'Spice' is buried here). Haggard visited Egypt in 1887 and again in 1904, when he met Howard Carter, then custodian of antiquities at Luxor. Howard, born in Kensington on 9 May 1874, was a sickly child and was sent to live with his aunts in Norfolk where his father worked on a painting for William Amherst of Didlington Hall at Swaffham and Howard accompanied him. Amherst was an Egyptologist who

Co-pilot, 1st Lieutenant Presley C. Broussard, pilot Captain Allen 'Ben' Alexander and navigator, 1st Lieutenant Thomas G. Kirkwood in front of the wreckage of *The Flying Crusader*, which crashed at Bradenham on 9 October 1944.

Liberator *The Last Frontier* in the 392nd Bomb Group at Wendling which crashed at West Bradenham near the base on 20 December 1943.

collected Ancient Egyptian artifacts and Howard became interested in this subject. The rest, as they say, is 'history'. In November 1922, Carter came upon the hidden treasure of King Tutankhamen while concluding his exploration of the Valley of the Kings. That same year Haggard finished writing *Queen of the Dawn*, a story of old Egypt.

On its return to Wendling on 20 December 1943 from an especially hazardous mission to Bremen B-24 Liberator *The Last Frontier* in the 392nd Bomb Group, which had lost two engines to flak was seen circling at low altitude. The flight engineer, Technical Sergeant T. E. Johnson of Clinton, Oklahoma was trying to force the nose wheel down when the other two engines quit. Interphone communication out, the pilot called out for a crash landing. Johnson crawled into the nose and pulled their trapped gunner out before stepping back into the bomb bay and throwing the gunner to safely onto the flight deck just before the B-24 crash-landed in a field on the Bradenham Estate. Johnson was trapped in the lower fuselage and died before he could be extricated.

At 1830 hours the next day *Miss Emmy Lou II*, a Liberator in the 44th Bomb Group which was part of a four plane practice formation, made a forced landing in farmer Percy Kiddie's field at Wood Farm after all four engines cut out. One member of the crew suffered major injuries and two others were sent home to the USA as hospital patients as it would take so long for their broken bones to heal in the English climate.

The peace and tranquility of the Bradenham Estate was not disturbed again until 9 October 1944 when Liberator *P-Bar Peter, The Flying Crusader* in the 392nd Bomb Group took off on a 'typical dreary, low ceiling day shortly after lunch' to test airborne radar apparatus and incredibly, crashed in the same field that had claimed *The Last Frontier* eleven months earlier! Technical Sergeant Frank E. Gallow the radio operator was killed.

Bradenham Hall's wartime chapter passed into history along with boyhood memories of Rider Haggard. The best-selling storyteller had moved to Ditchingham House, near Bungay in the next county where he died on the morning of 14 May 1925. Major Cheyne, Haggard's son-in-law, was with him the night before. 'The window blind was up and the blaze from a large building on fire was visible in the distance. Rider rose up in bed, pointed to the conflagration with arm outstretched, the red glow upon his dying face.'

'*My God!*' said Cheyne to himself, '*an old Pharaoh.*'

Many American airmen who embarked on missions from England died, like Tutankhamun, before they were twenty, never to see the fruits of their victory. And what of Bradenham Hall? In 1951, it was bought by Lieutenant Colonel Richard Allhusen and his wife Evelyn, who have lived in it ever since. In November 1992 two tragedies befell the stately home. On 9 November, burglars broke in and stole an invaluable collection of antiques. Later that same month 6,000 gallons of ammonia-based crop spray were washed into the River Wissey after the storage tank capsized. It was exactly seventy years after Carter had discovered King Tutankhamun's tomb.

Bradenham village sign depicting the English novelist, colonial administrator and agriculturist Sir Henry Rider Haggard, born 1856 in Bradenham Hall (died 1925).

Phantom light sources reported in control towers, pilots in full kit, faint tapping of Morse code coming from an empty building and telephone conversations heard in the ether are common on the old wartime bases. Lonely airmen waiting impatiently by roadsides for a lift that never comes are common apparitions. For several days, a car driver found himself giving a lift to a World War 2 pilot, who would suddenly appear in the back seat of his car when he reached a certain point of his journey. This stopped once the driver started taking a different route. On the B1052 leading into Hadstock, after losing his head in a flying accident, the apparition of an American pilot has been seen thumbing a lift on the roadside. At Great Waldingfield in Suffolk three men wearing long coats and large boots have been spotted on the road to Sudbury by a driver. Convincing they were going to hit one of the men, the driver slammed on their brakes; the figures vanished, leaving the witness quite shocked. The witness was later told that the area was a US air base in World War Two and that other people had encountered phantom airmen and even heard the sound of old aircraft in the area. At Harrington on the road leading to Lamport a car full of military personnel slowly fades from view as it travels the road. A man and his twelve year old son watched a hazy figure dressed in a World War Two uniform walking towards them, even though the figure did not appear to actually move closer. The uniformed man then reached down to the ground as if to pick something up and slowly faded away. People have seen an airman near the hangers and have also heard an air raid siren. Photographs taken are said to show a phantom figure. When farmers work the land where the WW2 airfield once stood, they are occasionally approached by a young man smoking a pipe who would wish them a good evening before vanishing. It was said that this ghost was once a pilot there.

At Burtonwood an airman has been observed standing around with no head – it is thought that he was decapitated as he tried to bail out prior to crash landing. At Cambridge Airport a number of buildings have reports of phantom pilots in their flying gear and RAF uniforms. Sounds of footsteps in empty areas are not uncommon and there is ghostly singing. During the 1960s there were a handful of reports of phantom aircrew at Bassingbourn, which was once used by the 91st Bomb Group. A B-17 may have been seen in 1994, moving silently overhead. More recently, a man who lived on the site of the former airfield reported seeing a pair of legs in dress uniform which manifested in his home and the sounds of aircraft starting up.

A witness who worked on a former bomber base site reported the smell of old aftershave in the corner of a warehouse which is only detectible at 20:30 hours and the sounds of young men in disused buildings. At Thurleigh airfield a man reported smelling a full English breakfast being cooked, though he was in the middle of an empty car park. He was told later that the spot was once the site of mess tents. The Officers' Mess is home to ghostly footsteps, while policemen patrolling the airfield once peered into an empty hut, only to see a group of wartime airmen playing cards!

At Duxford hangar 4 is a paranormal hotspot and some of the museum assistants will not lock up that hangar at night. There is a spirit that comes down the stairs of the office in hangar 4 but never reaches the bottom and there is reputedly a ghost pilot who walks from the hanger to the control tower. Other witnesses report hearing the sound of aircraft flying low overhead, though nothing can be seen. On 19 July 1944 John Putnam and Martin Smith had waited expectantly for the arrival of their buddy, Lieutenant James A. Sasser, a B-17 pilot at Horham, Suffolk. Sasser had been a member of the 84th Squadron at Duxford before joining the 95th Bomb Group. He appeared over the field in *Ready Freddie* with three other crewmembers on board. They landed and picked up Putnam and eight other members of his Squadron. Sasser then took off and proceeded to buzz the control tower at only a few feet above the flying field. Sasser judged his pull up over the tower accurately but evidently did not see the warning blinker light mast on top of the 84th Squadron's hangar behind the tower. *Ready Freddie* clipped the mast and the impact sheered off part of the left wing, which folded back and tore off the left horizontal stabilizer and part of the rudder. The B-17 rolled inverted to the left over the top of the Officers' Club, dropping the stabilizer on the lawn outside and the wing section on its roof while a fuel tank landed on an empty hut. *Ready Freddie* then passed over a corner of the ball fields at the back of the Club, causing the ballplayers to scatter and crashed into a main barrack block.

All thirteen men on board were killed. Smith, who died in the crash, had just eight hours remaining to finish his tour. Captain William J. Zink the Chaplain made two unsuccessful attempts to rescue Sergeant Ernest Taylor who was in the barracks. At first unable to reach him because of fumes and smoke, Zink dashed out, grabbed a gas mask and helmet and re-entered the building but falling beams and fire stopped him. Then he gave last rites for the

Ghosted image of ground crew working on a B-17 in the glass front of the American Air Museum at the IWM Duxford.

The tail section of B-17 *Liberty Belle* a composite B-17 constructed from two damaged aircraft and owned by 'The Liberty Foundation'. On 13 June 2011, shortly after takeoff from Aurora Municipal Airport in Sugar Grove, Illinois the wing was seen to be on fire and an emergency landing was made in Oswego where it was subsequently destroyed after the fire spread to the whole aircraft. It will be completely re-built.

victims and helped medical personnel extricate bodies from the wreckage of the bomber. He was presented with the Soldiers Medal for his actions and thus became the first Eighth Air Force chaplain to receive the award. Two others were badly burned. The barrack block burned for three hours until with the help of the Cambridge Fire Department, base firefighters finally managed to extinguish the flames. Had the accident occurred thirty minutes or so later, at least a hundred men would have been in the building having just come in off the flight line.

Many ghosts are said to exist at Bircham Newton. During the war, a car full of very drunk pilots crashed into a hangar, killing the driver and all the passengers; and can often be seen at irregular periods. Another group of ghosts appear in the old squash courts. The phenomenon began after a bomber crashed locally killing the crew. Apparently they had agreed that if anything should happen to them they would return to play their game of squash! The sound of a squash ball echoing in the deserted building and that of soft footfalls are more common than seeing the airmen, though one man in officer's clothing has been seen a few times. In the toilets is a permanent stain on the floor in the shape of a man and an airman in flying kit has been repeatedly seen there. A pilot killed when his new aircraft crashed into the sea was heard walking about his hut at night, his wet footfalls slopping on the floor.

At Tibenham an echoing voice has been heard barking orders at crews while using a non-existent tannoy. The voice is sometimes accompanied by the sound of a bomber warming up before take-off. At Elsham Wold a family living in the tower after the war reported hearing Morse messages being tapped out, seeing pilots dressed in flying gear and even once watching a large aeroplane taking off from the disused runway, baring the code letters 'PM'.

At Clacton-on-Sea in a disused sandpit and spinney two children have seen three pilots who are believed to be German; the sandpit being a crash site for a Messerschmitt 110. At East Kirkby (now an aviation heritage centre) a USAAF officer who is thought to have been killed when a Flying Fortress crash-landed near the site in 1944 has been seen several times on the runway, dragging his parachute behind him, as he slowly moves towards the control tower.

The WWII bicycles pictured in this 1970s' photograph of the inside the brick hut with the 'Flying Eight Ball insignia' at Shipdham now hang on the walls of Quarters Cottages and the emblem too has been preserved and framed and hangs with others of their ilk in the luxurious new cottages. As there was a shortage of rubber for inner tubes in WW2 the bicycle tyres were stuffed with straw.

At Honington between two barbed wire fences two RAF police officers spotted a man dressed in Second World War flying kit smoking a cigarette. When challenged, he walked through one of the fences and faded away. A local story reports that a USAAF bomber exploded on takeoff and one of the crew's bodies was never found.

At Langham in an apple orchard, the sound of a crashing aircraft has been reported amongst the trees and misty figures dressed in USAAF uniform have been seen – always dissipating when approached. Screaming was once heard coming from one end of a former runway, though when the sound was investigated, nothing was found.

Aerial view of the 14th Combat Bomb Wing HQ site where the completely refurbished buildings now have names like 'Lemon Drop Cottage' after the famous Liberator of the same name, 'Leon Cottage' in honour of General Leon Vance who was awarded the Medal of Honor for leading the 'Eightballs' on the raid on the Ploesti oilfields in August 1943, and 'Eightball House', while 'Wingate' is named in honour of the artist who originally painted the murals. (Author)

More than seventy years on the sun sets on an old control tower on one of the Fields of Little America. (Author)

Wartime MT building at Lavenham. (Author)

In November 1993 at Little Walden airfield near Saffron Walden, Captain Scholz, a Mustang pilot, who crash-landed at the base in WW2 and was killed, appeared in the back seat of a car dressed in his flying suit as it drives past the airfield. The apparition was only visible for a few seconds.

At the former Liberator base at North Pickenham in 1959 the sound of old aircraft engines, warming up, was reported coming from an empty hanger. At Framlingham (Parham) airfield, which is now a museum, locals have reportedly heard the droning of phantom aircraft, while the control tower has reappearing 'wet footprints', which begin and end in inexplicable places. One woman reported seeing the reflection in glass of a man in USAAF uniform who smiled at her. The lady said 'hi' and turned to the figure, but no one was there. At Raydon near the former Officers' Mess, a ghostly Military Policeman is said to walk the area. There are also reports of phantom aircraft, including a P-47 and a B-17. At Ridgewell airfield the area is haunted by the sounds of crashing WWII aircraft, airmen shouting and other noises. (The same thing happened to some friends of mine at Snetterton.)

In an actual incident a Fortress in the 91st Bomb Group that was on a mission to the Merseburg oil targets received a direct hit that put the #3 engine out of commission and another hit to the centre of the plane just before reaching the target area. The B-17 was unable to remain in formation and, in addition, the bomb racks were malfunctioning. 'We've taken a direct hit in the bomb bay,' said pilot Harold R. DeBolt 'and for the life of me I don't know why the bombs didn't blow up.'

With bad weather coming and one propeller twisted, DeBolt knew they could not make England so headed for Brussels and ordered the

Lavenham control tower on a winter's day. (Author)

Wartime art work displayed on stairs said to be haunted by a ball turret gunner takes on a ghostly appearance at Thorpe Abbotts Control Tower Museum.

Yesterday, upon the stair,
I met a man who wasn't there
He wasn't there again today
I wish, I wish he'd go away...

American poet William Hughes Mearns (1875-1965)

The mural of B-17G 43-38877 in the 325th Squadron Ready Room in the 92nd Bomb Group at Podington, which was a piggery when this picture was taken and was the scene of a 'haunting' long before it was extracted whole and displayed at Duxford, where, unfortunately it was repainted and thus lost for all time any authenticity it might have had.

crew to ditch all loose equipment to lighten the aircraft. It was at this time that two engines stopped. DeBolt ordered the crew to bail out while he put the B-17 on automatic pilot. He was the last one to leave the plane. The crew all landed safely and, believe it or not, so did their stricken B-17! Twenty minutes after the B-17 landed, the propellers continued whirling, but nobody disembarked from the plane. As emergency crews climbed aboard and looked around; to their shock and surprise, they found no one inside.

There are several other accounts of B-17s that flew without a pilot, but DeBolt's phantom Flying Fortress is the only one that ever landed successfully, more or less intact – by itself! Or was it?

At Bury St Edmunds (Rougham) on 5 January 1944 B-17 *L'il Butch*, which was shot down during a bombing run on Bordeaux and all seven crew killed, briefly reappeared later at the air base, as if it had just landed, before disappearing forever once again. (There was also a B-17 named *Ghost of a Chance* at the base in WW2.)

More recently an investigation by six members of the 'New World' paranormal team was setting up CCTV equipment in a room at the Rougham Control Tower Museum after reports of 'spooky happenings' but when a female member of the team snapped a photo, they were stunned to spot a mysterious figure of an airman at the bottom of a stairs. The team also claim to have recorded a ghost calling out the surname of one of their female investigators in a dark, demonic voice. When part of the group tried to communicate with the spirit it only responded to one of the ladies. (*Over-sexed, over-paid and over-here?*) Officers from Suffolk Police have apparently seen apparitions of dead servicemen at Rougham too.

In the late 1980s Peter Worby, an 8th Air Force researcher, experienced a ghost on the stairs of the control tower at Thorpe Abbotts, the 100th Bomb Group's base in WW2. The ghost was Corporal Homer L. Parish whose spirit would not leave him. On 11 July 1944 the 'Bloody Hundredth' had just returned from a raid and Parish, who was the ball turret gunner on one of the B-17s, was killed outright as he ran for cover when one of the guns he was clearing suddenly started firing over 200 rounds in all directions.

At Podington in Bedfordshire in the 1990s Peter and a colleague were digging up pieces of the crash site of a B-17 piloted by Jack Pearl which crashed on take-off on 20 May 1944 killing all ten crew. The scene was very eerie as they both had the feeling that they were being watched. However no-one was there.

If there are ghosts they surely haunt the East Anglian wartime airfields. I was a long time disbeliever in anything 'ghostly' and like most everyone else, 'pooh-poohed' any notion of such a thing. However, this all changed in the early eighties. Pauline Neale, living in Northamptonshire wrote to say that she was planning to visit the 2nd Air Division Memorial Library in Norwich and 'would I meet her?' She liked my book *Fields of Little America* and wanted to 'pick my brains' as her knowledge of the subject was limited. We met up at the library and she began pumping me for answers to questions like 'what was a P-51' and 'flak'? etc. She said she was a 'medium' and had 'picked up' (my words) a story about a 392nd Bomb Group Liberator crew at Wendling in Norfolk that had been killed when they crashed in the Friesian Islands returning from a mission. The pilot had apparently signed out a jeep the night before so that he and his co-pilot and the bombardier and navigator could enjoy a night on the town. The bombardier or the navigator, who said that they would 'chauffeur' the pilots for a change, knocked down and killed or injured a local who was riding a bicycle in the dark. As the jeep was booked out to the pilot, he got the blame. A policeman arrived next morning to take a statement but the Liberator crew did not return and that was the end of it.

Sometime later I received a cassette tape recording and this story took an eerie turn. Pauline and her husband were making a long journey home in their car one evening when the tape recorder, which was in her briefcase on the back seat, turned itself on and recorded the engine sound and an argument they were having. The tape begins with a 'spooky' rendition of *John Brown's Body* and then strikes up with the running sound of the car except that it is more akin to an aircraft; and the argumentative voices sound like males! Suddenly, the tape ends with the engine sound cutting out and it is replaced by a 'swooshing' noise like an aircraft with no power diving to its doom. An eerie voice (Pauline's) says: 'the wing has gone'! The 'whooshing' sound is the Liberator gliding down into the sea (off the Friesians), 'the wing has gone' means 'out of fuel' and the engines have stopped.

I still have the tape if anyone wants to hear it but I suggest you do not listen to it alone in the dark! One night my brother-in-law did and with eyes watering, he bolted!

Sometime later Pauline said she was visiting Podington airfield and would I like to meet up? I duly arrived and found that she had gathered an entourage of three or four local lads, who knew the base history backwards. My knowledge however was scant; Pauline's even more so.

B-24 Liberator *Arise My Love and Come With Me* in the 458th Bomb Group at Horsham St Faith.

She drove her car and we followed in mine. Nearing the entrance to the old base she suddenly stopped, got out and, white-faced, pointed to a field nearby where she could 'see' GIs playing baseball! The lads affirmed that it was used for this purpose in WW2. Then she said 'there's a sentry post over there and there is a guard in naval uniform'. I told her that this was an 8th Air Force base not navy' and turned to seek confirmation but the lads, now white faced themselves, said, 'this was an *anti-submarine base* before the 8th Air Force arrived!

Pauline stopped her car abruptly two or three times more, once when she heard 'STOP!' It transpired that she was about to cross the overgrown main runway, where planes used to land and take off in WW2.

When she stopped again it was at a grassy patch near one of the brick barrack huts. 'Chow!' she exclaimed – it was site of the old Mess Hall; long since demolished!

The piece de resistance was the 12-foot wide 8-foot high mural of an airborne B-17 that had been painted on a wall inside the old 325th Squadron Ready Room in 1945 by Staff Sergeant George C. Waldschmidt a Squadron bomb aimer or 'togglier'. The art work had been rediscovered in the late sixties when the building became a piggery. Trying to photograph it Pauline's Polaroid camera flash failed and so I suggested we synchronise on mine: 1-2-3-click. Her photo began appearing like a ghostly image in half brown and half blue with a faint outline of the '17 mural. She said 'Angus!' but did not know why. Two weeks later Pauline phoned to say that she had visited Madingley Cemetery and found a 'Bill' Angliss! (While researching for this book I found that Private 1st Class William J. Angliss, ball turret gunner on B-17E *Baby Doll* crashed into the Channel on 6 September 1942. There were no survivors.)

In Norwich some years later two men laying floors in a newly erected industrial unit in Barker Street just off Heigham Street, quite near to where I live had apparently been 'spooked' by an apparition inside the building, which was empty save for themselves. They heard footsteps, stopped work and looked up to see two airmen in flying clothing walking towards them! The both downed tools and ran for the exit!

Some years later I entertained a gentleman wanting information on quite a different matter but towards the end of the evening he suddenly asked if I knew about historical events that might have happened in the Heigham Street area in WW2. His daughter lived in one of the new flats in Freeman's Buildings, which had been built on the opposite side of Heigham Street about the time some pre-war terrace houses were demolished. Apparently she was in her bath one night when an airman in 'old flying gear' appeared!

Father and daughter were quite unaware that in November 1944 a Liberator in the 458th Bomb Group at Horsham St Faith (now Norwich Airport) which had hit the tower of a local church and careered low over the city, had crashed in the old Corporation Yard behind the terrace houses in the exact same spot where the industrial unit now stands, killing all nine crew.

The plaque in their memory that had been affixed to one of the terrace houses in 1945 was moved to its present site on the side of a wall at Freeman's Buildings in 1972 when Heigham Street was redeveloped!

The Heigham Street plaque pictured in its original location having been erected in 1945 to all the members of a Liberator crew in the 458th Bomb Group at Horsham St Faith (now Norwich Airport) who perished when their bomber crashed in the old Corporation Yard nearby. (Author)

8. THE STATELY HOMES OF THE EIGHTH IN ENGLAND

'Me and my crew of My Gal' had arrived in the middle of the afternoon with a low ceiling and visibility measure in yards. We had heard about the comfortable bases the 8th had in England; old mansions etc., but it didn't take long to see that Rattlesden was another of the Army's SNAFU (Situation Normal, All Fouled Up) jobs – so we bought galoshes and waded in. We had been wading ever since. The barracks were concrete, roof, rafters, walls and floor and damp.'

1st pilot Martin J. 'Jack' Gruber, 447th Bomb Group at Rattlesden near Felsham, Bury St Edmunds.

Sometimes referred to as 'The house guests from hell' the higher echelons of the USAAF and RAF as well as hospital patients and men billeted in the grounds, were accommodated in thousands of requisitioned country houses. On the whole, the airmen of all nations treated their palatial lodgings with respect but tales abound of soldiers using Old Masters as dartboards and staircases for firewood. Men from twelve successive battalions from nine regiments made Melford Hall in Suffolk and the Nissen huts in the park their home. The owners returned after the war to discover the wine cellar had been raided. The soldiers had drunk all the wine and refilled the bottles with water, replacing the corks to look as if nothing had happened.

Elveden Hall, which was purchased in 1894 by the 1st Earl of Iveagh of the Guinness brewing family, was used as a headquarters for the US Third Air Division in WW2. There is evidence to suggest that the staff quarters were struck and destroyed by a bomb. (Author)

Curtis E. LeMay, who as commander of the 4th Bombardment Wing, was promoted to Brigadier General in 1943 and transferred to command the 8th Air Force's 3rd Bomb Division which had its headquarters at Elveden Hall. In August 1944 he was transferred to the China-Burma-India theatre as leader of 21st Bomber Command.

'I had the privilege of working with General Curtis E. LeMay when he was commander of the Third Air Division in 1943 with his headquarters at Elveden Hall. Our War Room was a big former bedroom on the first floor. One evening at dinner in the Officer's Dining Hall we noted he General was sporting a second star. We got up and applauded. All he said was, "I think that this will increase my income tax!"'

2nd Lieutenant James Renton Hind,
Combat Intelligence Staff Officer.

Memorial stained glass window to the Third Air Division in Elveden church created by Hugh Easton.

WAC Corporal Geraldine Hill receives reports on aircraft positions in the plotting room of the 3rd Bomb Division at Elveden Hall in February 1944. Geraldine lived in Texas all of her life and worked for more than thirty years as a bookkeeper for the Baptist General Convention of Texas. The war brought an interruption to her career when she volunteered as part of Dallas's civil defence and then when she enlisted in the Woman's Army Corps. She served overseas for twenty-seven months both in England and continental Europe.

Instructions on doors in Elveden Hall still visible today.

The water tower at Elveden Hall with washing hanging out to dry in the foreground. Camp Blainey was probably a camp of tents and/or huts used to house the staff, erected in the grounds of the Hall. Much of the location filming for the *Dad's Army* took place in Breckland and the Thetford area and the water tower once featured in a memorable episode of the hit BBC series.

Lieutenant Helen Pierson, an army nurse based at Wimpole Hall, christens a B-17 Flying Fortress of the 91st Bomb Group at Bassingbourn named *Lady Helen of Wimpole* in her honour. Helen later married Major John D. Davis, Commanding Officer of the 401st Bomb Squadron at the base.

From 7 July 1944 to 1946, Wimpole Park was the home of the 163rd General Army Hospital reporting 1,266 beds (inclusive of tents). The facility received its first patients on 5 October 1944. It later became an assembly centre for American patients from the other eight US Army hospitals in the immediate area who were being sent back to the states (Zone of Interior). The remaining patients of the 121st Station Hospital, located in Braintree, Essex were evacuated to the 163rd GH during the first week of June, 1945. The majority of these patients were surgical cases.

Opposite: Spitfire 'Scramble' at Duxford.

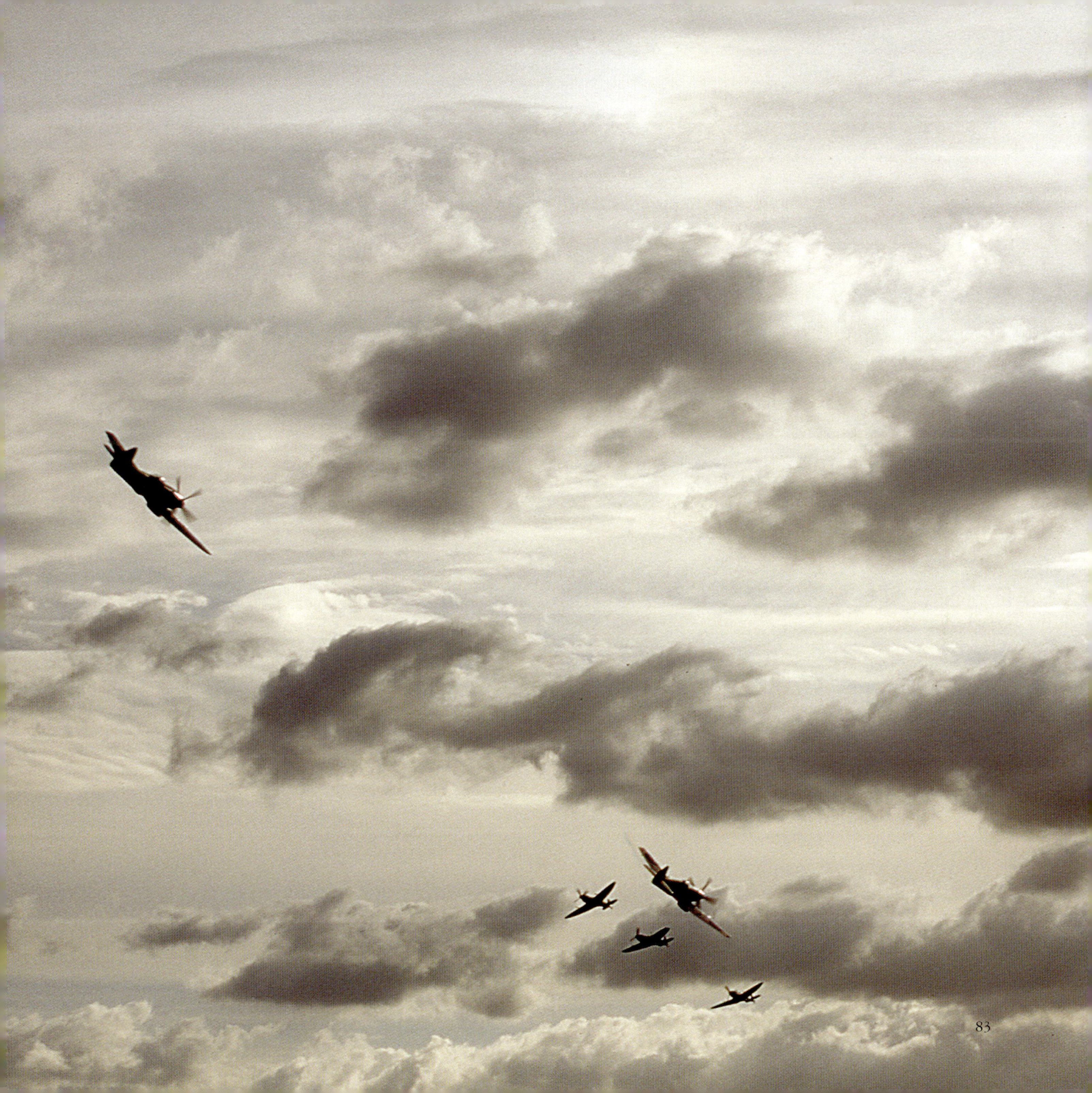

9. 'ARTISTIC LICENSE'

'The mail sent over for us to censor for skipping a squadron meeting and lecture on customs and behaviour governing military personnel and British civilians is in three canvas mailbags filling up our room and we stumble over them... I read one letter out of a square blue envelope. It's from a guy who can't wait for the war to end, so he can go home and give it to Dearest Thelma over and over again their special way. A few minutes later I find another square blue envelope from the same guy wanting to give it to 'Dearest Gladys' their special way. We rummage through the bag for square blue envelopes. We find four more. "Dearest Patsy", "Dearest Violet", "Dearest Dorothy" and then jackpot – "To My Darling Wife Harriet".'

A Real Good War, Sam Halpert.

When George Petty, Alberto Vargas, Gil Elvgren and other talented artists created their stunning girls, no doubt these men had no idea how far their talent would reach. Not only would it dominate World War II nose art, but it would travel across the decades to the present and find itself being applied to modern military aircraft.

Each of these men had, as one would expect, a love of the feminine form. When George Petty sat down to create his almost aerodynamically sleek girls, he used live models, particularly his daughter, whose facial features can be recognized in almost every painting. Though the *Esquire* 'Petty Girl' was famous in her own right, Petty was just as well known for his long association with Jantzen since he painted most of their swimwear ads using the same airbrush techniques.

When Alberto Vargas emigrated from Peru and started to walk the streets of New York, he was smitten with what he considered to be the most beautiful women he had ever seen. He decided to devote himself to painting them, which led to contracts with the Ziegfeld Follies and several movie studios. His excellent portraits of 1930s' Hollywood movie stars opened the door to *Esquire* where the magazine dropped the 's' from his name and created the Varga Girl.

Gil Elvgren was famous in his own right for painting the soft, warm Coca-Cola ads of the 1940s and 1950s. He never used live subjects per se, but would take pictures of models in various poses he had in mind, then paint from the photos. His series of popular pin-up calendars across several decades are immediately recognizable to anyone who used to visit car parts stores or blue-collar repair shops.

The History of Aircraft Nose Art WW1 to Today by Jeffrey L. Ethell and Clarence Simonsen (Foulis Aviation 1991)

'Ed' Hennessey's crew of B-17 *Little Audrey* in the 306th Bomb Group at Thurleigh receiving a blessing from Father Adrian Poletti, the Group Roman Catholic chaplain. The Group had two Fortresses with this name during the war.

One of the ways an airman could express his love and thoughts of home, or of American womanhood, was to have his favourite pin-up, or his girl-friend, wife or fiancée painted on the nose of his aircraft, often in nude form. B-24 Liberator *THE SHACK* in the 493rd Bomb Group at Debach was a clever pun which referred to Ann Shackleford; pilot Captain David L. 'Doc' Conger's fiancée. *THE SHACK* was transferred to the 458th Bomb Group at Horsham St. Faith (now Norwich Airport) in the late summer of 1944 when the Third Division groups converted to the Fortress. Conger and his crew flew their last mission of their tour on 14 January 1945.

B-24 Liberator *NOV SHMOZ KA POP?* in the 446th Bomb Group at Bungay (Flixton). Two Fortresses, one in the 94th Bomb Group at Bury St Edmunds (Rougham) and 487th Bomb Group at Lavenham were similarly named. Cartoonist Eugene Ahern's comic strip *The Squirrel Cage* (1936-53) featured a bearded character known as 'The Little Hitchhiker', who became notorious for his frequent expression, *Nov shmoz ka pop?* which he uttered while thumbing for a ride. Some sources say that the phrase is Russian for 'Going my way?' while others claim that the phrase is complete nonsense.

'Returning to base, I was sent to Liverpool depot to ferry some replacement B-24s to Hethel. I got a Ford-built B-24J and signed for her. We checked her over and took off. At Hethel I discovered that she was assigned to me with a new crew chief, Sergeant Svec. He came to my barracks one evening with a roll of paper. "Skipper, I've got a proposition, I've got a friend, Sergeant Michael Otis Harris, a painter who wants to paint a nose-art picture on our new ship to top them all," and he unrolled the picture. A beautiful nude artistically posed, but blonde. I said, "OK Svec. Tell him it's a deal if the price is right – and if that blonde becomes a brunette."

"Skipper, the price is right. He just wants to do it, for free."

"OK Svec, the name is *'Delectable Doris'* and I had to write it down for him to make sure."

The painting was done in record time.'

Bill Graff, pilot, 389th BG, Hethel

'Bill' and Doris Graff pose for the camera in front of B-24 Liberator *Delectable Doris*.

B-24 Liberator *BOOBY TRAP* in the 490th Bomb Group at Eye (Brome) in Suffolk. There were at least three Fortresses in the 8th Air Force with this name.

Major Byron Trent in the 490th Bomb Group at Eye (Brome) with B-17 *Bobby Sox* which was originally purchased by War Bond donations from employees of the Springfield Armoury. Painted by Sergeant Jay Cowan, his superb graphic style created a memorable image which contains his signature in the shadow just below the sock held in the beautiful nude's right hand. In May 1945 the veteran Fort was chopped up for scrap at Walnut Ridge, Arkansas.

'We both mooch around the magazine rack and he shows me a picture in Modern Screen *of Ida Lupino in a sexy, low cut, tight nurse's uniform with her knockers about falling out as she bends toward us waving a banner reading For Our Brave Lads Overseas. ... Both* Time *and* Look *are featuring articles about how the war will be over by Christmas. I pick* Life *which has Rita Hayworth on its cover flexing in a negligee damn near showing it all. I flash it at Cavey. "Eat your heart out" I say. He takes a deep breath and says, "Now that's what I call qualified quail, but way too rich for your blood, bad for your pimples." He riffles through the pages of* Sensational Hollywood Starlets *of 1944 and shows me a two page picture of the healthiest sweater girl I've ever seen. "Oh man" he says "those mallomars sure make a guy proud to be American; they belong carved up there on Mount Rushmore..."*

'He flips the pages to Marie ("The Body") McDonald smiling at us in short red tights and a white angora sweater with a blue ribbon marked Miss Victory '44. He moans as he turns the picture around bit by bit; squinting his eyes, checking every curve and angle.

"How can we lose?" he asks.'

A Real Good War *by Sam Halpert.*

'The finest writing to come out of the war so far, according to John Steinbeck, special writer for the *New York Herald Tribune*, is the illustrated literature appearing on the fuselages of the Boeing Fortress, Consolidated Liberator, North American Mitchell and Martin Marauder bombers of the Army Air Forces abroad. The thinking behind these names and illustrations is inspiring to read because it represents the very essence and spirit of the young, hell-bent-for-election American crews who fly and fight these ships and endow them with their own personalities.

'The names, anecdotes and art work appearing on these war planes are so American that soldiers in the Far East, in Africa and in England get homesick all over again looking at them. The names bring back home memories of the familiar comic strip characters syndicated in home town newspapers from coast to coast – *Corky, Superman, Popeye* and the ever popular animals of the cartoon shorts shown in US movie houses – the Disney characters and that geared, carrot-chewing rabbit with the Bronx accent who is a very popular figure on the noses of our combat airplanes. The wise-cracking inscriptions and names also bring back memories of the Hit Parade tunes, the double talk of high school days and their girls – *Vibrant Virgin, Pistol Packin' Mama, Paper Doll* and just plain "Mary", "Helen" and "Joho".

The great majority of the bow decorations seen on the Liberator and Fortress bombers today still carry the female theme, but nowadays little or nothing is left to the imagination. The girls are all-American from their blond wavy curls to tinted toenails. They generally lie in languorous postures with arms under their heads and long, fascinating legs extending horizontally toward the pitot masts – reclining in sun-bathing position and costume. These fine girls are all unusually well developed specimens – a combination of the best features of the Varga and Petty girls, only with less clothing and executed on a scale large enough to make an infantry soldier's mouth water when the ship passes overhead even a thousand feet above...'

'What's In a Name?' by Captain Stanley Washburn, *Stars and Stripes* 1944.

B-17 *COMMANDO CHIEF* in the 306th Bomb Group at Thurleigh. Two other Fortresses in the Group were called *Piccadilly Commando*, which had an entirely different connotation.

After a competition was held by the US Forces newspaper *Stars & Stripes* to find 'the most beautiful WAC serving in England', the resultant vote saw Pfc Ruby Newell declared the winner. Pfc (Private First Class) Newell was a member of the Women's Army Corps and her likeness was painted on a 385th Bomb Group B-17 Flying Fortress at Great Ashfield by artist Corporal William Ploss and named *Ruby's Raiders*.

B-17 *Bit o' Lace* in the 447th Bomb Group was named by Milt Caniff who responded to a request for permission to use his popular comic strip personality *"Miss Lace"* and Corporal Nick Fingelly used his considerable skill to apply suitable art to the nose, which finished the war with a total of 83 missions flown. When the Fortress was finally flown to the breaker's yard at Kingman, Arizona, Fingelly was amongst the skeleton crew on board.

FLAMIN' MAMIE which was assigned to the 'Bloody Hundredth' Bomb Group at Thorpe Abbotts on 4 December 1944. On 5 April 1945 it was force landed at Dole in France but safely returned to the USA on 20 June 1945.

B-17 Fortress *Boston Bombshell* in the 91st Bomb Group at Bassingbourn. The Group had two Fortresses with this name – 42-39898 failed to return (FTR) on 22 February 1944 and 42-39996 FTR on 16 August 1944.

B-17 *Miss Gee Eyewanta* (Go Home) in the 401st Bomb Group at Deenethorpe, which put down at the B-24 Liberator base at Wendling where this photo was taken.

Wall murals at the 305th Bomb Group's Officers Club at Chelveston painted by Captain Charles Bruce Bairnsfather, a prominent British humorist and cartoonist whose best-known cartoon character is 'Old Bill'. 'Bill' and his pals 'Bert' and 'Alf' featured in Bairnsfather's weekly *'Fragments from France'* cartoons published weekly in *The Bystander* magazine during the First World War. He was hospitalised with shellshock and hearing damage sustained during the 2nd Battle of Ypres. In WW2 he continued 'Old Bill' work, but was not asked to help with the British war effort. Instead, he became official cartoonist to the American forces in Europe, contributing to *Stars and Stripes* and *Yank* magazine, whilst residing at Cresswell House in Clun, Shropshire. He also drew cartoons at American bases and nose art on aircraft.

At Chelveston Bruce Bairnsfather applied his 'Old Bill' cartoon both to the mess wall and to the nose of a B-17.

'The Wet Lounge' in 'The Red Feather Club' at Horham in Suffolk.

'A Nissen hut at Hethel' one of a series of wartime watercolours by Technical Sergeant L. Lund in the 389th Bomb Group in 1943.

'We were flying somebody else's plane, the *Keystone Mama*. I turned my flashlight on the brown lady with no brassiere, painted on the side and decided they were short of artists at this base.'

Serenade To The Big Bird, Bert Stiles. (*Keystone Mama* failed to return with Lieutenant Robert S. Wylie's crew on 19 May 1944. Eight crew were KIA, one was made POW.)

99

'Grim-faced Luftwaffe pilots, proud of the guts that take them within the suicide circle of a Fortress formation, determined to do or die for the Fatherland, must wonder what the hell kind of an air force they are up against. They come driving in, teeth clenched, hell-bent for Hitler and along with a hail of lead they are greeted by the stupid grin of some absurd comic-book character, or the nude form of a "Petty girl" painted on the nose of the bomber they are attacking.

'Most of the 8th Air Force bombers operating from England have fantastic names scrawled across their elongated noses. Many of the names are illustrated by out-of-this-world characters, in brilliant colours, which could only originate in the minds of the men of one air force.

'The Forts aren't named for any particular reason and no one in particular names them, it is a very American process.

'A pilot from Maine is apt to come out any rainy morning and find that his plane has been named Texas. Or the quiet teetotaller who quit divinity school to join the air force is apt to come out on the line and find a nude stretching from the plastic nose to the pilot's compartment, because his tail gunner (who did not quit divinity school to join the air force) knew a guy in Site Six who used to be a commercial artist in St Louis and could still draw a plenty sexy nude.

'The names of many Forts and Libs are famous in America. Not all the exploits of the men and the bombers they fly are buried under their plane numbers in the files in Washington.

'... The Fort, *We The People*, has been on at least thirty-two raids and she has never had a single man aboard wounded. The most remarkable part of the ship's story is that the same ten men have never flown the bomber twice. Altogether *We The People* carried 114 men over enemy territory in her first thirty-two raids. Originally the ship was christened *Snafu* and was considered a jinx plane, but the record is one of the best in the ETO.

'It would take a shipment of paint to cover the Fort names you wouldn't kick around in your living room, but the order fell flat and the names stand. If the brass had been up on their 'Li'l Abner', as they should have been, the whole episode might not have occurred...'

***Stars and Stripes*, 'Nudes, Names and Numbers',**
Andrew A. Rooney, 5 August 1943.

Souvenir programme from *Skirts* – an intimate musical in fourteen scenes which played at 8th Air Force bases and theatres in England.

Mason And Dixon, a long serving Flying Fortress at Thorpe Abbotts was named after two 100th Bomb Group Officers, pilot Floyd Mason and navigator William Dishion, the racy semi-nude painted by Sergeant Frank Stevens made use of some clever script to avoid censorship. Note the airship shed at Pulham in the background. The first operational coastal airship was delivered to the site in August 1916 and they became known as 'Pulham Pigs' from their yellowish-buff envelope.

B-24 Liberator *The Spotted Ape*, which was stripped of all armament and carried no bombs and was employed by the 458th Bomb Group at Horsham St Faith as an 'assembly ship' to form up the group over Norfolk and send them on their way before landing back at base.

B-17 *Humpty Dumpty* in the 100th Bomb Group with the superb artwork by Sergeant Frank 'Steve' Stevens whose workshop was close to hardstand six at Thorpe Abbotts where the ground crew worked on the Fortress. Stevens based his design on 'Forced Landing', one of the famous Gil Elvgren creations in the Brown & Bigelow calendar. *Humpty Dumpty* was one of the twelve B-17s that FTR on New Year's Eve (not for nothing was the Group known as the 'Bloody Hundredth'). All nine of the crew – on their 13th mission – survived.

Liberator *El Toro - Bull of the Woods* in the 446th Bomb Group at Bungay (Flixton) who came to be known as 'the Bungay Buckaroos'. This Liberator survived the war and was flown home to the USA where it was scrapped along with the thousands of other surplus bombers.

The alluring nose art of *Kentucky Belle* in the 446th Bomb Group which also survived the war and if there was any justice, should have been saved for display in a museum (or even an art gallery?).

(Albert Krassman collection)

104

Wistful Vista in the 446th Bomb Group which was salvaged on 30 June 1944 after a crash. (Albert Krassman collection)

Un-named nose art depicting 'Donald Duck' toting a machine gun on a B-24 in the 446th Bomb Group.

B-17 *MOUNT 'N RIDE* which was assigned to the 91st Bomb Group at Bassingbourn on 1 February 1944. It went MIA (Missing in Action) on the mission to Augsburg on 16 March when after losing two engines it was force landed at Dübendorf in Switzerland.

B-17 *Goin' My Way* in the 100th Bomb Group, one of nine bombers so-named in the 8th Air Force.

Lady Geraldine in the 100th Bomb Group at Thorpe Abbotts survived her combat tour and was scrapped at Kingman in the Arizona desert 'boneyard' in December 1945, which unfortunately was the fate of almost every single B-17 and B-24 that was now surplus to requirements.

Piccadilly Lilly II followed in the footsteps of the original *Piccadilly Lilly*, which was one of the most memorable Fortresses in the 100th Bomb Group, if not the entire 8th Air Force but which was lost in combat on 8 October 1943. *Piccadilly Lilly II* was salvaged on 27 June 1944.

In the passing years many hundreds of 8th Air Force veterans including these in 389th Bomb Group who were in Norfolk to look over their old air base at Hethel and the town of Wymondham, visited their old haunts. They are standing in front of the 'Green Dragon' public house, which gave its name to the green- and yellow-striped assembly ship used by the 'Sky Scorpions'.

Fightin' Sam in the 389th Bomb Group at Hethel. (John J. Driscoll)

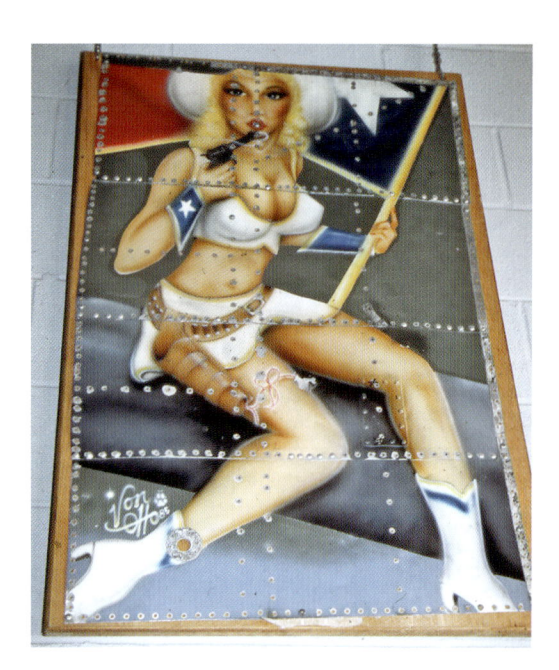

B-17 *Texas Raiders* in the days before the Confederate Air Force was renamed the Commemorative Air Force and the eye-catching risqué nose art favoured by the GIs was removed and replaced with a stylized and fully clothed figure.

Sally B, now even more beautiful than before.

It's *Witchcraft*! The original Liberator flew in the 467th 'Rackheath Aggies' Bomb Group near Norwich

112

113

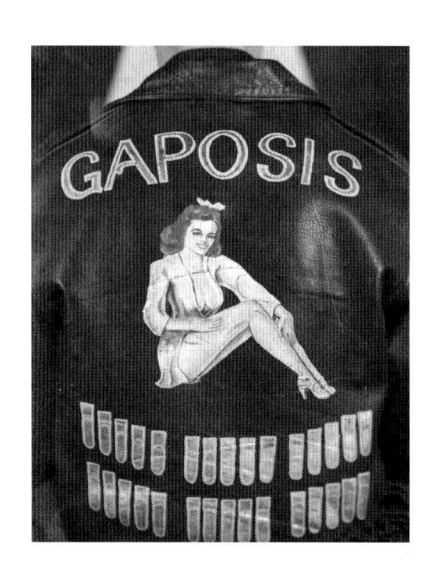

114

B-17G *Texas Raiders*, which was given this name in 1967 during its 1960s restoration when this 'Fort' was part of the Confederate Air Force (now the Commemorative Air Force) in formation in October 1986 with PBJ-1J Mitchell *Devil Dog* and B-17G *Sentimental Journey*, which was used as a water bomber until 1978 when it was donated to Arizona Wing of the CAF. (Author)

10. FLYING TO VICTORY

'We learned after the war that Hermann Goering said he knew the air war was lost when he saw the bombers over the capital with their P-51 escorts.'

General 'Jimmy' Doolittle

The P-51 Mustang was designed from the outset to satisfy RAF requirements and only afterwards was it taken into service with the USAAF. The first Mustangs reached Britain in 1941 and when they finally entered service with fighter squadrons pilots' morale soared.

Another American import that helped build morale enormously was Edward R. Murrow, head of CBS European Bureau in London. Murrow's reports, especially during the Blitz and later aboard aircraft on bombing missions over Germany earned him undying fame and his phrase *'This is London'* became synonymous with the newscaster and his network. He often broadcast from rooftops as bombs fell on the city. But he also told countless stories about the daily life that goes on during a war. They were stories about ordinary people during extraordinary times.

'Even for those of us who live on the crest of London, life is dangerous. Some of the old buildings have gone, but the ghosts, sometimes a whole company of ghosts, remain. There is a thunder of gunfire at night. As these lines were written, as the window shook, there was a candle and matches beside the typewriter just in case the light went out.'

A week later he reported: 'I'm standing again tonight on a rooftop looking out over London, feeling rather large and lonesome. In the course of the last fifteen or twenty minutes there's been considerable action up there, but at the moment there's an ominous silence hanging over London. But at the same time a silence that has a great deal of dignity.'

One of Murrow's most famous broadcasts came on the night of 24 August, 1940. He began his report with the words, 'This...is Trafalgar Square.' Murrow described the scene from the steps of the St Martin-in-the Fields church with the sound of air-raid sirens in the background. A microphone captured the sound of footsteps on the sidewalk, as people walked slowly along the street to a bomb shelter below. He said the footsteps sounded 'like ghosts shod with steel shoes.' Murrow saw a red double decker bus driving by. In the darkness, the lights from inside the tall bus reminded him of a ship passing in the night. He observed a bright search light beam reaching straight up into the sky.

Murrow's CBS radio broadcasts continued until the end of the war in 1945.

Flight of Fantasy. A Spitfire with a Hurricane behind over *92 Squadron*; a 'Battle of Britain Class' locomotive 'flying' along the North Norfolk Railway line towards Sheringham. (Author/Mike Page)

Trafalgar Square was famous as a home for thousands of feral pigeons. A popular activity was to feed them but this made them even more of a pest. So, in 2003 the Lord Mayor of London banned feeding the pigeons (and the selling of feed near the square) and a hawk was employed to keep them away. Slowly, the pigeon population began to decline and now concerts and public events can be held in the square. (Author)

Have you ever sat in Trafalgar Square Beneath the morning sun, in the morning air? Have you looked at the lions 'neath Nelson's feet And watched the traffic pass by in the street? Have you seen the people taking their time While Big Ben sounds out its hourly chime?
I'm sitting here now and it thrills me to see A preview of peace. How good it will be!'

Private first class Sidney Jrueger writing in *Stars and Stripes*.

CBS War Correspondent 'Ed' Murrow who in 1940 broadcast live from the steps of St Martin-in-the-Fields on the corner of Trafalgar Square during a German air raid on London.

Lieutenant Herman C. 'Mitch' Mitchell a Liberator pilot in the 93rd 'Travelling Circus' Bomb Group at Hardwick feeding the pigeons in Trafalgar Square in 1945. On 8 May the famous London square was invaded by thousands of people to listen to Winston Churchill's historic broadcast and celebrate VE Day. Mitchell's crew had completed their combat tour just after D-Day, 6 June 1944. All except three of his crew returned to the States and received a 30-day leave. One became a briefing officer and Mitchell remained in England where he and the radioman delivered much needed fuel to the troops in France and Germany. Mitch's drinking brought on by combat stress ultimately led to alcoholism when he returned to the USA and he died aged 46 in 1969.

'We take a cab down to Piccadilly and amble around the cold, gray late afternoon. Hundreds of pigeons soar over us as we walk through Trafalgar Square. "What a piss poor formation," I say. Earl cups his hands over his mouth, tilts back his head and yells "Tighten 'er up goddam it, tighten 'er up, where the hell did you guys learn to fly?" Another squadron of birds takes off as we come near them. We watch them assemble as they circle overhead. A white stain with a small yellowish green centre lands splat on Earl's sleeve. He shakes his fist and swears at the pigeons, then turns to me. "See, I told you we had it made. We're in the clear." He points to stain and says "this always means good luck back home…"

'Later, in a Hungarian restaurant in old Soho two damn birds are skin and bone. As we walk through Trafalgar Square again Earl says "I'll bet if they do a count, for sure they'll come up with a pair of missing pigeons…"

A Real Good War by Sam Halpert.

'BERLIN, May 5 1945 (delayed) – Berlin, the capital of defeat, today is the charred, stinking, broken skeleton of a city.

It is impossible to believe that the miles of disembowelled buildings, or crater-pocked streets, of shattered masonry once could have been the capital of Greater Germany and the home of four million people.

Only a handful remain as the last clatter of-machine-gun fire echoes through the hollow city. There are no factories left for them to work in, no shops, no theaters, and no office buildings.

But the handful are busy. They are shovelling the rubble from the streets, sweeping the dead out of the way – working while the Russian conquerors walk the streets with straggling columns of prisoners or wander around staring at the shells of once-great buildings of state.

The Russians are everywhere. Their tanks rumble through the great Tiergarten Park. A pert girl MP smartly directs traffic at Unter den Linden. An infantry battalion forms in front of the shrapnel-scarred statue of Wilhelm the Great. Soldiers wander in and out of cellars. Cavalrymen wash their horses at the edge of the Spree River.

Cossack Rides Along

A Cossack rides down the Wilhelmstrasse raising a cloud of dust from the powdered stone and concrete that, despite the rain, coats everything.

In front of the bomb-hollowed Reichstag high-ranking Russian officers gather. Atop the Reichstag's hole-filled dome a torn Red flag flies. In the circle which is the center of the Tiergarten a group of Soviet soldiers pose for a picture in front of a statue of the haughty Moltke. A band plays and Russian soldiers dance to native songs in the great place before the Opera.

Unter den Linden, which a 1929 guide book proudly calls the "most beautiful avenue in all the city," is gray with the universal powder of death and broken as all the rest. The street is still the "gathering place best known to foreigners." Today, except for two American soldiers and a few "slave" laborers from western Europe, the foreigners are battle-dirty Russians, walking slowly with slung tommy-guns or pushing down the streets in convoys of US-made jeeps and trucks, honking constantly. No one is buying anything from the "smart shops, catering to the most elegant tastes." The shops are closed permanently.

A Hurricane

The trees in the Tiergarten – Berlin's zoological park – looked as though a hurricane had ripped through the city. Shell-shredded, half leafless, they are as broken as the buildings. A Red parachute dangled from a smashed branch. The hull of a burnt-out Panther lies beneath a fallen trunk. Twisted barrels of 88s and 75mm anti-tank guns mark the remains of dug-in positions along the parkway.

Beside long columns of Red-flagged Russian tanks are smashed six-barreled, self-propelled mortars, trucks, sedans.

Nearly intact is the great Brandenburg Gate – Berlin's triumphal arch and symbol of its military glory. Its columns still stand,' their bases partly blocked with debris. On top, one age-green bronze horse pulls the chariot of Victory, but the chariot is smashed and Victory is only mangled metal. One of the horses has fallen to the ground.

On the Wilhelmstrasse, the Reichs-chancellery is gutted, as are all the buildings where the Nazi great made their plans to make this street the nerve center of the world. No one seems to know if Hitler's body is in the Chancellery. No one seems to care.

On Wallstrasse the entrances to the Berlin subway are choked with broken concrete and timbers. Smoke rises from a new fire in one of the already-burned buildings down the street. The bridges over the Spree slump into the water, but a few civilians, their possessions loaded on baby buggies, make their way across a corner of the span. The Russians are at work repairing one bridge.

On Lindenstrasse, a rider-less saddled horse picks his way among the debris. At the Belle Alliance Platz, the graceful statue dedicated to the Beautiful Alliance stands high on its slender column in the midst of ruin. Russian soldiers are eating lunch on the low stone wall that surrounds the statue.

That's what it's like as you tour the city, mortally wounded by Allied bombers and finished off in a street-by-street fight whose dead men, guns and tanks make its only tombstones. All you see are rubble and Russians.

It's the same in all districts, residential, industrial, business. Only some of the suburbs are still alive and they are scarred and damaged. The smells of sewage and death are everywhere.

As you ride out of Berlin, on the one wall that remains in a whole block near the city's southern limits, you see a sign, whitewashed into the crumbling bricks. It says, "Mitt Unser Führer, Zum Sieg". Translated that means, "With Our Führer We Shall Be Victorious."

Berlin's Ruins Symbolize Complete Nazi Defeat by Ernie Leiser *Stars and Stripes* Staff Writer, Friday, May 11, 1945.

A pockmarked and bullet-scarred wall in Berlin 72 years after the bloody Russian advance into the German capital in 1945. (Author)

VE (Victory in Europe) Day! Inset: 'Gwendolyn' and 'Penelope', two 'Piccadilly Commandoes', join in the VE Day 1945 celebrations in Piccadilly Circus.

Two airmen from the 490th Bomb Group base at Brome walking along the bedecked streets of Eye in Suffolk on VE Day.

*The ghost of an air gunner flew to heaven
Arriving soon at the locked Heavenly Gate
Where Saint Peter, the custodian was waiting
To determine the ghost air gunner's fate*

*"Let me in" pleaded the ghostly air gunner
"Tell me why I should" Saint Peter replied
"You have not been a fine example of virtue
Many times you have strayed or have lied"*

*"I know" cried the ghost of the air gunner
"But I hope that all of my sins you'll forgive
Though at times I have not led a chaste life
An air gunner's life is not easy to live"*

*"At times I drank too much in the canteen
And told sweet lies to a pretty young maid
In an attempt to ease the fear and tension
That are present on each bombing raid"*

*"I caroused with crewmates when on furlough
To church only on church parade would I go
Sometimes breaking some of the Commandments
Charity on my fellow men I'd not always bestow"*

Saint Peter And The Air Gunner from
'No Place To Hide' by George 'Ole' Olson RCAF
during his tour of operations 1943-45

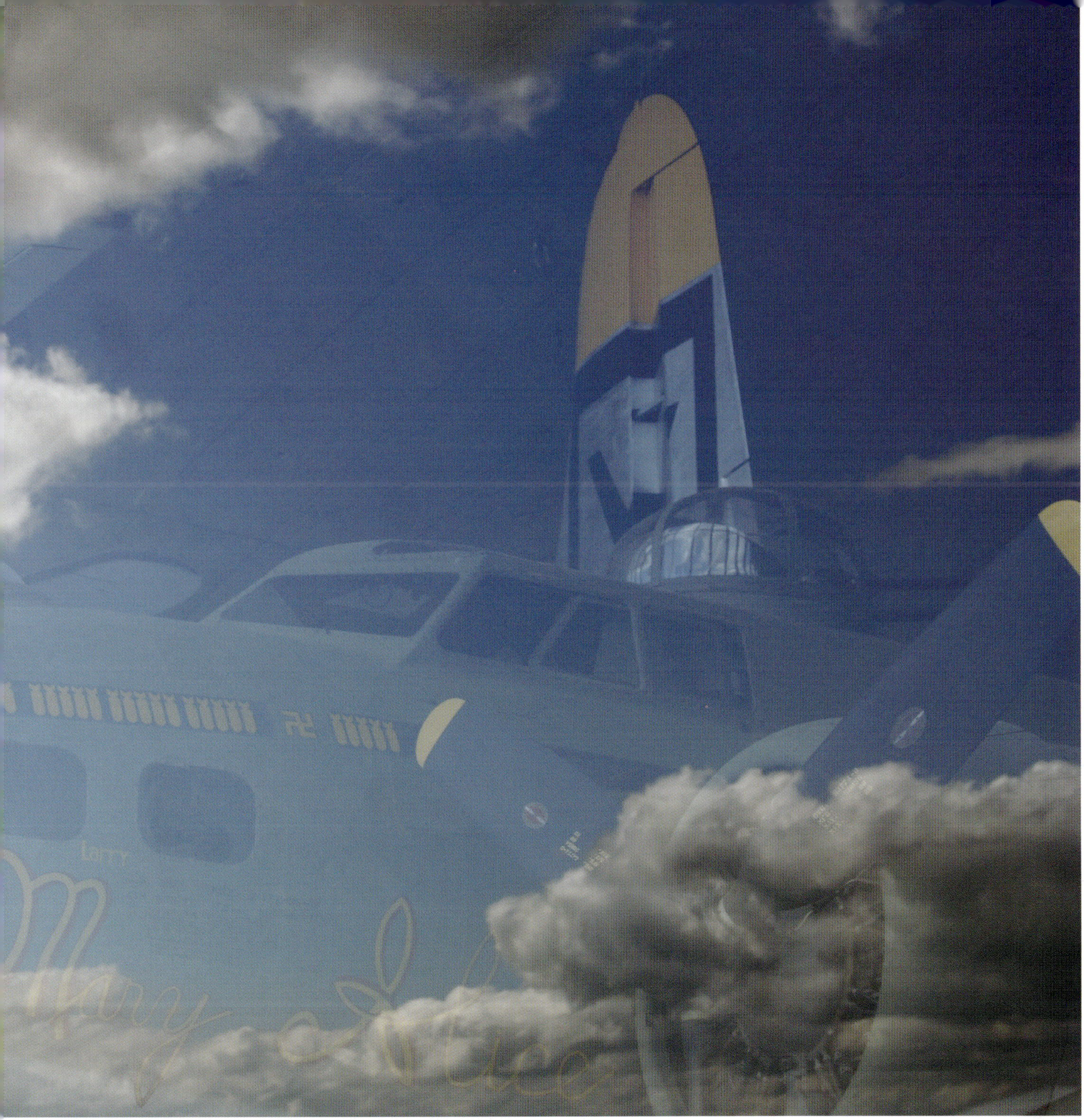

VERNACULAR

Two Great Nations divided by a common language.

George Bernard Shaw

ARs – Army Regulations

Barracks Bag – duffle bag containing things most immediately needed

Barracks Lawyer – soldier who thought he knew Army law

Bird Colonel – full colonel

'Big Friend' – bomber

Bitch – to complain, or a complaint

Bombardier – bomb aimer

Brown Nose – to toady, or one who toadies

Buzz – to fly low

Chow Hound – man fond of eating

Chow Line – mess queue

Close Order Drill – square bashing

Dear John – a letter from a girl back home saying she's found someone else

Dogface – infantry soldier

Dog Robber – batman

Draftee – conscript

Dry Run – rehearsal

Duck – amphibious truck

ETO – European Theatre of Operations, i.e. Britain

ETOUSA (pronounced 'Eetoosah') – European Theatre of Operations, United States Army, i.e. Britain

First John – first lieutenant

First Sergeant – company sergeant major

First Soldier – first sergeant

Flak Happy – state of victim of aerial battle fatigue

Fly Boy – anybody in the Air Corps

Four by Four – four-wheeled vehicle with four- wheel drive, usually a jeep

French Bath – sponge bath in a GI helmet

Full Bull – full colonel (in the Air Corps)

Funny Money – Sterling

Furlough – leave

GI ('Government Issue') – an American soldier

GI Jane – member of US Women's Auxiliary Army Corps

Gl Joe – soldier

GIs – diarrhoea

Hash Mark – service stripe

Holy Joe – chaplain

Hot Crock – contemptuous expression for nonsense, untruth, exaggeration

Ike Jacket – GI battle jacket (patterned on Eisenhower's)

Jeep – General Purpose vehicle

Junior Birdman – to ground troops any airman, but to fliers a new, inexperienced pilot.

Kraut – German

Latrine Lawyer – barracks lawyer

Latrine Rumour – unfounded rumour

Latrinogram – latrine rumour

Leaf Colonel – lieutenant-colonel

Light Colonel – lieutenant-colonel

'Little Friend' – fighter plane

Maggie's Drawers – red flag waved on a rifle range to indicate that target was unmarked.

Milk Run – easy, routine bomb run, or any routine, easy job

Night Fighter – Negro GI

Ninety-Day Wonder – product of OCS

No-ball target – Air Corps nickname for a German rocket launching site

Non-com – NCO

OCS – Officer Candidate School

OD – officer of the day, or olive drab (both the colour and the uniforms themselves, e.g. 'I'm wearing my ODs tonight.')

Over the Hill – AWOL

PFC – poor f......civilian, or private first class

Piccadilly Commando – prostitute

Pill Roller – medic

Poop – information (i.e. 'What's the poop from the group?')

PX – Post Exchange, nearest equivalent of NAAFI

Red-lined – cancelled or classified unserviceable

Repple Depple – Replacement depot

Re-tread – old officer recalled to active duty

Rugged – arduous and unpleasant

Sack – bed

Sack Alert – stand-by air crew's assignment

Sack time – bedtime, or sleep

SCH- 'safe course home' – the compass course given to USAAF fighter pilots to get them back to Britain if their radios broke down.

Scrubbed – cancelled

Second John – second lieutenant

Section Eight – discharge given for mental instability, inability to adjust to service life, or insanity

Section Eighter – man bucking for Section Eight Discharge

Shack Job – easy woman

Shack Up – to sleep with woman

Shipping Out – departing

Shortarm – VD inspection

Six by six – six-wheel truck with six-wheel drive

Sky Pilot – chaplain

Snafu – 'Situation normal, all fucked up'

Snowball – military policeman

Snow Job – exaggeration or downright lie, usually to cover up something

SOS – (Shit On a Shingle) creamed chipped beef on toast, or Services of Supply

Spam Medal (or ribbon) – ETO ribbon

SNAFU – Situation Normal, All Fucked Up

Tarfu – 'Things are really fucked up'

Top Kick – first sergeant

Tough Shit – tough situation

TS Card – Tough Situation Card, issued by any chaplain desperate to appear to be one of the boys

USO – United Services Organisation, nearest equivalent of ENSA

V-Mail – letters to or from home, reproduced photographically to conserve shipping space

V-Packet – GI prophylactic kit

Whore Bath – same as French bath

'You found a home in the Army!' – taunt aimed at any GI who seemed satisfied with anything in the Army

Zled – sent home (to the Zone of the Interior, i.e. America)

In Memoriam

Sam Halpert, born Brooklyn in 1920, an apprentice typesetter from Buffalo was a navigator on the crew of *Mah Ideel* in the 91st Bomb Group, flying the required 35 missions. His defining novel, *A Real Good War* was written at the age of 77. It has been described as 'engrossing', 'gritty, funny; rich with authenticity and gutsy realism'. Nontogenarians' 'Larry' ('Goldie') Goldstein and Wilbur Richardson, too, contribute to this salute dedicated to the Eighth Air Force.

ACKNOWLEDGEMENTS: Barrie and Lesley Adams of 'Quarters Cottages'; John Carter; Muriel Colborn; the crews of *Sentimental Journey* and *Texas Raiders*; the late John J. Driscoll; Arthur Edward Rory Guinness, 4th Earl of Iveagh; the Red Feather Club, Horham, Suffolk; the late Sam Hurry; the late Beirne Lay Junior; The New York International Air Show; Nigel McTeer; Mike Page; Gordon Richards; the staff of the 2nd Air Division Memorial Library, Norwich; Robert J. Shoens; Carol and Ron Batley of The 100th Bomb Group Memorial Museum; the late General Paul W. Tibbets; Jo Redfarn and the *Sally B* team; Roy West and Karen Binaccioni at Halsgrove.